Between Them

Parker, Richard, and Edna, New Orleans, V-J Day 1945

Between Them

Remembering My Parents

Richard Ford

An Imprint of HarperCollins*Publishers*

HarperCollins books may be purchased for educational, business, or sales promotional use. For information please e-mail the Special Markets Department at SPsales@harpercollins.com.

FIRST EDITION

Designed by Suet Yee Chong

Library of Congress Cataloging-in-Publication Data has been applied for.

ISBN 978-0-06-266188-3 (hardcover)

ISBN 978-0-06-268825-5 (B&N signed edition)

17 18 19 20 21   RRD   10 9 8 7 6 5 4 3 2 1

Kristina

In writing these two memoirs—thirty years apart—
I have permitted some inconsistencies to persist between the two, and I have allowed myself the le-
nience to retell certain events. Both of these choices,
I hope, will remind the reader that I was one person
raised by two very different people, each with a separate perspective to impress upon me, each trying to
act in concert with the other, and each of whose eyes
I tried to see the world through. Bringing up a son
who can survive to adulthood must sometimes seem
to parents little more than a dogged exercise in rep-
etition, and an often futile but loving effort at con-
sistency. In all cases, however, entering the past is a
precarious business, since the past strives but always
half-fails to make us who we are. RF

Gone

Remembering My Father

Parker Ford (date unknown)

Somewhere deep in my childhood, my father is coming home off the road on a Friday night. He is a traveling salesman. It is 1951 or '52. He's carrying with him lumpy, white butcher-paper packages full of boiled shrimp or tamales or oysters-by-the-pint he's brought up from Louisiana. The shrimp and tamales steam up hot and damp off the slick papers when he opens them out. Lights in our small duplex on Congress Street in Jackson are switched on bright. My father, Parker Ford, is a large man—soft, heavy-seeming, smiling widely as if he knew a funny joke. He is excited to be home. He sniffs with pleasure. His blue eyes sparkle. My mother is standing beside him, relieved he's back. She is buoyant, happy. He spreads the packages out onto the metal kitchen table top for us to see before we eat. It is as festive as life can possibly be. My father is home again.

Our—my and my mother's—week has anticipated this arrival. "Edna, will you . . . ?" "Edna, did you . . . ?" "Son, son, son. . . ." I am in the middle of everything. Normal life—between his Monday leavings and the Friday nights when he comes back—normal life is the interstitial time. A time he doesn't need to know about and that my mother saves him from. If something bad has happened, if she and I have had a row (always possible), if I have had trouble in school (also possible), this news will be covered over, manicured for his peace of mind. I don't remember my mother ever saying "I'll have to tell your father about this." Or "Wait 'til your father comes home. . . ." Or "Your father *will not* like that. . . ." He confers—*they* confer—the administration of the week's events, including my supervision, onto her. If he doesn't have to hear it when he's home—ebullient and smiling with packages—it can be assumed nothing so bad has gone on. Which is true and, to that extent, is fine with me.

HIS LARGE MALLEABLE, FLESHY FACE was given to smiling. His first face was always the smiling one. The long Irish lip. The transparent blue eyes—my eyes. My mother must've noticed this when she met him—wherever she did. In Hot Springs or Little Rock, sometime before 1928. Noticed this and liked what she saw. A man who liked to be happy. She had never been exactly happy—only inexactly, with the nuns who taught her at St. Anne's in Fort Smith, where her mother had put her to keep her out of the way.

For being happy, however, there was a price. His mother, Minnie, an unyielding immigrant from County Cavan, a small-town widow and a Presbyterian, maintained views that my mother was a Catholic. Why else go to their school? Catholic meant "wide" instead of diffident and narrow. Parker Carrol was her youngest of three. The baby. Her husband, my father's father—L.D. Jr.—was already a suicide. A dandified farmer with a gold-headed cane in a small Arkansas town. She'd been left with all his debts and his scandal. She meant to protect her precious last. From the Catholics, definitely. My mother would never fully own him, if his mother had a say. And she would.

My father did not project "a strength," even as a young man. Rather, he projected a likable, untried quality, a susceptibility to being over-looked. Deceived. Except by my mother. From my memory, I know he tended to stand back in groups, and yet to lean forward when he spoke, as though he was expecting soon to hear something he'd need to know. There was his goodly size; the warm, hesitant smile. A woman who liked him—my mother—could see this as shy, a fragility a wife could work with. He would likely not disguise things or himself: a man who wasn't so *knowing* that you couldn't take care of him. There *was* the terrible temper, not so much anger as eruptive and impulsive, born of frustrations with things he couldn't do or hadn't done well enough, or didn't know—private dissatisfactions, possibly of the sort that had made his young father take a seat on the porch step one moonlit summer night in 1916, having lost the farm to bad invest-ments, and poison himself to death out of dismay. My father's temper wasn't of that kind. His sweet-ness, the large forward-leaning sunniness and un-certainty worked against that, allowed an opening for a life my mother could see and enter with the sound of her name. Edna.

When she met him, she was seventeen. He was possibly twenty-four—a "produce man" at the Clarence Saunders grocery in Hot Springs, where she lived with her parents. It was a small chain of stores, now gone. There is a photograph I have: my father, standing in the store with the clerks— wooden bins all around, brimming with onions, po-tatoes, carrots, apples. It is an old-looking place. He is wearing his white bib apron and staring, slightly smiling for the camera. His dark hair is neatly combed. He is ordinarily handsome, competent-appearing, alert, a young man on the way to some-where better—a career, not merely employment. It is the twenties. He has come to the city from the country, equipped with farm virtues. Was he ner-

Parker, Hot Springs, Arkansas, 1929

vous in this picture? Excited? Did he fear he might fail? Why, one wonders, had he left tiny Atkins, where he was from? The world's pickle capital. All of it is unknown to me. His brother, Elmo—called "Pat" for the Irish lineage—lived in Little Rock, but soon went to the navy. His sister was at home with a burgeoning family. Possibly, by the time of this picture, he had met my mother and fallen in love. Dates are no more clear than reasons.

Not long after, though, he took a better job managing the Liberty Stores in Little Rock—another grocery chain. He joined the Masons. Though soon, robbers would enter one of his places of business, wave guns around, take money, hit my father in the head, and depart. After which he was let go and never told precisely why. Possibly he'd said something he shouldn't have. I don't know how people saw him. As a bumpkin? A hick? A mother's boy? Not brave enough? Possibly as a character to whom the great Chekhov would ascribe a dense-if-not-necessarily-rich interior life. A young man adrift within his circumstances.

Time then, and another job—in Hot Springs,

again. He was married to my mother now. The thirties were beginning. Then another, even better job came—selling laundry starch for a company out of Kansas City. The Faultless Company. I don't know how he gained such a job. The company still exists in KC. To this day there are pictures of my father on the walls in the offices, with other salesmen of that time. 1938. This job he kept until he died.

With this work came a traveling territory—seven southern states—plus a company car. A plain Ford tu-dor. He would "cover" Arkansas, Louisiana, Alabama, and a small part of Tennessee, a slice of Florida, a corner of Texas, all of Mississippi. He was to call on the wholesale grocer companies that provisioned small stores across the rural south. He arrived at each and wrote down orders for starch. There was only the one product. His customers occupied murky, back-street warehouses with wooden loading docks and tiny stifling offices that smelled of feed by the bushel. Piggly Wiggly and Sunflower and Schwegmann's were the big accounts. He liked his small customers best, liked arriving to their offices with something he could make happen. A sale.

Many—ones in Louisiana, across the Atchafalaya—
spoke French, which made it more difficult but not
impossible. No one hit him in the head.

HE WAS NOW ON THE ROAD ALL THE TIME, and my
mother simply went with him. Little Rock would
be home—a small two-room apartment on Center
Street. But they *lived* on the road. In hotels. In Memphis at the Chief Chisca and the King Cotton. In
Pensacola, at the San Carlos. In Birmingham, at the
Tutwiler. In Mobile, the Battle House. And in New
Orleans at the Monteleone—a new city to them,
very different from what they'd known in Arkansas. They loved the French Quarter—the laughing
and dancing and drinking. They met some people
who lived in Gentilly. Barney Rozier, who worked
on oil derricks, and his wife, Marie.

Part of the traveling job was to attend "cooking schools" in the small towns. Young girls came
out of the backwoods to learn to be wives—to cook
and clean and iron, to keep a house. Guard armor-
ies, high school gymnasiums, church basements,

Elks Clubs were where these took place. He and my mother worked as a team, demonstrating for the girls the proper way to make starch and use it. It wasn't hard. The Faultless emblem was a bright red star on a small white cardboard box. "You don't have to cook it" was the company motto. There was a song with that phrase in it. My father had a tolerable tenor voice and would sing the song when he'd had a drink. It made my mother laugh. He and she—barely out of their twenties and exceedingly happy—handed out little boxed starch samples and cotton hot pads to the country girls, who were flattered to receive such gifts at a time when nobody had anything. The Depression. It was enough to get them started and to make a lasting impression when they went to the Piggly Wiggly. The car's back seat was full of hot pads and samples.

Imagine it. You have to, because there's no other way: this being their whole life. On the road with no great cares. No children. Family far away. My father wore a felt hat in the winter and a straw one in summer. He smoked—they both did. His face was assuming a maturer look—again, the Irish lip, the thin mouth, and thinning hair. He had an awareness of himself. He was on his way—almost suddenly—to being who he would be. He experienced some trouble with his teeth that necessitated a bridge. A partial. He was six foot two and had begun to take on weight—above two-twenty. He owned two suits, a brown and a blue, and adored his work, which agreed with his obliging nature. About himself, he said he was "a businessman." His boss—a Mr. Hoyt—trusted him, as did his customers in all the tiny towns. He didn't make a lot—less than two hundred a month, with expenses. But they didn't spend much. And he'd found a thing he could do. Sell. Be liked. Make friends. The military wouldn't be a worry. A heart murmur had been detected, and his feet were flat. Plus, his age— too young for the first war, too old if a second one started, which eventually it did.

The two of them began to know more people— on the road, other salesmen encountered at wholesale grocer conventions or at the cooking schools or in hotel lobbies. At the Carousel Bar at the Monteleone. By the duck pond at the Peabody in Memphis. Ed Manny. Rex Best. Dee Walker were these men's names. They traveled for Nabisco and General Mills and P&G, or for his "competitors," Argo and Niagara. It was collegial, more or less.

There certainly wasn't reading. There wasn't television, only the car radio. There wasn't air-conditioning for the car *or* the rooms. Only ceiling fans and the window if there was a screen. There *were* movies, which my mother liked, but he didn't care about. They ate in supper clubs and bars and roadside joints, had breakfasts in hotel coffee shops and diners. For my father, behavior and awareness ran on a single track. There wasn't much looking to the side of things. It made for a *present* he liked.

For Faultless he was regularly the low man in gas consumption and the thriftiest in expenses charged back. He drove a steady 60 mph—the most economical way to drive. There was no hurry. He didn't wish to lose his job when jobs were scarce. They were together everywhere, all the time. Each Sunday morning, wherever they were—in some hotel—he wrote out his expense reports in the room or at the little *escritoire* in the lobby, his tiny, barely decipherable ink-pen scratchings filling the forms the company provided. Then he walked to the post office and mailed off a fat envelope to Kansas City. Special delivery.

All along they wanted children. It was the normal thing. But that simply hadn't happened. They weren't sure why. Though it only made them closer—walled out the past and the future both. A suicide for a father and a severe Irish mother can close off a lot. Plus, my mother had had anything but an easy life before going to the nuns. The *past* for them wasn't an accommodating site. As for the future and intimacy, they would be each other's *givens*. He had his job and relied on her. She could do figures, could conceptualize, think of things he couldn't. She was lively and watchful. If they talked about dreams, what they would do or later seek, what was out of reach, what they remembered and regretted, what they feared, what delighted them—and of course they did— there were no records kept, no letters, diaries, no notes on the backs of photographs. It wasn't thought necessary.

SOMEWHERE BEHIND THEM, of course, there *was*
his difficult family and hers. My mother was pretty,
black-haired, small, curvy, humorous, sharp-witted,
talkative—and therefore difficult to accept in Atkins, though no one precisely said so. From his
mother they kept a distance, even when they visited,
and even though they slept in her house, the house
left by the scandalous father, up the hill from Atkins with a view down to the highway and up Crow
Mountain. His mother thought of her son differently
now—as if he'd acquired airs with this new, possibly Catholic wife; had embraced ambitions; had met
people one didn't meet if one were from where he
was from. The country. They'd been married by a
justice, not in church. All was acceptable, but nothing precisely was. His sister loved him, her many
children adored him, called him—Parker Carrol—
"Uncle Par'Carrol." But all was under the mother's
ceaseless eye. She kept her counsel, waited, ruled
what she could rule, but did not mean to receive the
new "daughter."

For *my* mother, there were added matters to
dwell upon—given her life, overseen by her own

rattily Ozark parents. Her people were from the sticks—worse than the country. North Arkansas. Tontitown. Hiwasse. Gravette. Way up there. My father had not known such people growing up. My mother's mother was only fourteen years older than her daughter, and was punitive, jealous. She'd divorced the father. He was gone. The pretty, blond-headed second husband/stepfather, Bennie Shelley, was a quick-witted gigolo—a talker, a club boxer, a railroader, a show-off—but a man with a future, whom my mother's mother, Essie Lucille, intended to hold on to, even if it meant sending her vivacious, smiling daughter off to the convent school in Fort Smith when things with Bennie grew unwieldy. Which they did. At least until the two of them needed the pretty daughter to bring in a paycheck, at which point they took her out of school at sixteen and put her to work, too young, in the cigar stand at the Arlington Hotel in Hot Springs, where Bennie now oversaw the catering department. Again, it was the Depression. They needed to salt money away. They were not to be held back.

For her, though—Edna—my father's family

might've been a *real* family. Irish or not, country or not, narrow with pieties, suspicions and misfortunes—all that set easily enough to the side. Had his mother been the least bit welcoming, my mother might've found more than enough to fit into. She was, after all, likable—knew it about herself. The sister liked her—privately. The cousins did. My mother could make you laugh. She knew interesting things the nuns had taught her. Plus my father loved her. What could be wrong? No one was making great demands. It should've been better. She wasn't a Catholic. But nothing was forthcoming.

So it became with *her* people—my mother's and not his—that they forged a bond. She at least knew *them*. And there were attractions. They drank—illegally. Bennie smoked cigars, played golf, wore spectator shoes, hunted ducks with wealthy men, told jokes, knew women, lived it up to a certain extent—though was cautious not to inch above his station. He was an Arkie. They all three were. Knowing your place—who you were above, who below—was second nature. He called Essie "Mrs. Shelley" because in the hotels where they worked—at the Huckins in Oklahoma City, at the Muehlebach in KC, the Manning in Little Rock, the Arlington—that was the protocol, even if you were married.

They were her parents, but there was little difference in their ages—the four of them. 1895 was Essie. 1910, my mother. Bennie and my father were in the middle—1901, 1904. They all "went out" together in Hot Springs and Little Rock. Roistered. Arkansas had been a state less than a hundred years, and Little Rock was the center of things, the capital—a characterless, rowdy, self-important, minor river town. Neither south nor west, not quite middle west. More like Kansas City or Omaha than Memphis and Jackson. There were streetcars, new bridges, big department stores owned by Jews, restaurants, gambling on the sly, Main Street movies, new hotels. Booze, in spite of Prohibition. Things were *going on* in Little Rock. They had all four been drawn to there from their own private nowheres.

What my father, a big, courteous stand-offish young husband, felt about Essie and Bennie, I don't know. He may have gotten swept up a bit. The world was slightly new to him and always would be. Certainly it was odd to have your in-laws be *these* people: on the one hand, your contemporaries; on the other, a sensation that they were in charge. They liked him without much knowing him. She stood between him and them and buffered things. His having married Edna, taken her away and made her happy was a convenience—especially to her mother. There was a bawdy, amiable, loose-limbed ruthlessness to the parents, a rough-trade aura affiliated with ambition. They were big personalities. They had scrapped beyond life in the boondocks, while my father was a traveling salesman from sixty miles up the road.

And it was all much more than I'm saying. You can be sure. What I don't know can't rightly be called a feature of who he was. My father. Incomplete understanding of our parents' lives is not a condition of *their* lives. Only ours. If anything, to realize you know less than all is respectful, since children narrow the frame of everything they're a part of. Whereas being ignorant or only able to speculate about another's life frees that life to be more what it truly was.

My father was almost, but not completely, a *kind* of man by then. Not a boy. Yet not a full-scale adult. A husband, a wage-earner certainly, a son, a brother, an uncle. But among the four of them, as a son-in-law, he was 4th. He didn't recede as much as *settle* into a role within their small hierarchy. He may have realized it. His large size and politeness, which made people like him—these may also have bottled him up. As if mannerliness was a measure of not being prepared for life. It would be the pattern around the three of them—his being 4th. Though it could also have been that for all he was—reticent, not quite gainly, smiling, forward-leaning, newly married, loved and in love—it might've been the most exquisite time of his life.

BEING BOTH A *LATE* CHILD and an *only* child is a luxury, no matter what else it might be, since both invite you to speculate *alone* about all the time that went before—the parents' long life you had no part in. It fascinates me to think of the route their life *could've* followed that would've precluded me: divorce, even earlier death, estrangement. But also greater closeness, intimacy, being together in a way that defies category. They more than certainly had *that* in them. They wanted me; but they did not need me. Together—though perhaps only together— they were fully formed.

They stayed on the road. Life went on as it had, from the thirties straight into the forties. They owned little—a bit of furniture, their clothes, no car. My father grew larger, lost more hair, smoked too much, remained a star in his selling work. They traveled to Kansas City for sales meetings. They came to New Orleans often and thought it could be a place to live. It had an open feel. He didn't long for Atkins, though he managed a visit to his mother when he was nearby. He went hunting with the cousins, doted on his nieces and nephews. He gained stature at home. They all, except the mother, learned to like Edna—if not entirely, at least in the ways they liked certain surprising sides of themselves. She was too pretty and lively and irreverent not to be semi-accepted. One merely avoided certain subjects. It wasn't hard. And *he* loved her, which was what mattered.

The war began. His brother went and so did two nephews. He had the heart murmur and did not go. It must've been odd for life to carry on in a normal way while the terrible fighting took place overseas. It might've been a thing he regretted—missing the chance to come back changed. Some abstract, un-uttered thought—something he may not have noticed—could've coursed through his mind, made him think of himself differently. As being less competent. Or just lucky. Or both.

What were their frustrations, my mother's unspoken wishes? What did they say to each other in the car during all those traveling miles alone? He had become thirty-six, she was thirty-one. He must've become fully a "kind" of man now. An adult. A salesman with a wife. He affected few people beyond her and his customers; though affecting people would not be a part of what life meant to them. Did he "develop"? Feel more confident? Did this way of floating begin to seem old? Was there an extra dimension to their life where before there hadn't been? Is it bad if there wasn't?

It's revealing—though perhaps only of oneself—to think of people in terms of what might've been better for them. The writer who might *better* have been a lawyer; the lawyer who might *better* have been a teacher; the soldier who might *better* have been a priest; the priest who might *better* have been most anything. My father could've sold something else. Cars. He could've worked in a hardware. Possibly he could have farmed with his father, if he'd had one. But he wouldn't likely—in my view—have done much better than he did at Faultless. He had no notable skills besides his good personality. Selling was perfect. His job—fitting into it and liking it—was part and parcel to understanding him. Greater challenges might only have frustrated him and rendered him unhappy. If he had dreams of something else, I never heard of them later. He seemed to be where he belonged and thought so. If he had a self-image, his own outlook, it was *that*. Habit became his guide—along with my mother. It does no injustice to him to say that.

BUT THEN, TO EVERYONE'S SURPRISE, my mother was pregnant in the summer of 1943. And the course of everything changed.

Seeing one's advent as a mixed blessing is not necessarily bad. They had almost certainly concluded—after fifteen years—that there would be no children. My parents may have harbored complex and possibly unexpressed feelings about that: of life now staying the same—and being good. Of settling somewhere—just the two of them. New Orleans. The time together was precious. It was what they knew. Did he feel he had something to impart that, without a child, would never be imparted? Did each or both of them think my father would not live long due to his heart so that a child was a needless difficulty? All are possible.

As I said, they officially wanted children. Though that they were now *going to have a baby* could only have been unsettling. He'd become thirty-eight and was not robust. She was thirty-three. His boss in Kansas City—Mr. Hoyt again, who had children of his own—said, "Parker, you have to choose a place to live now. Not just the road. Find the middle of your territory. You can be home more." This seeking may have been what was happening anyway.

Yet if there was ever going to be a job change—to a hardware in Little Rock, or back to stocking lettuce, or a return to Atkins—this would've been a moment. The Depression was behind them. The war was on, but would be over. Better times were possible. But there was no thought of changing that I ever heard about. The selling job was too good. And he was too good *at* it. Instead, they would choose a place—in the middle, as he'd been told—and live there. Being on the road together for those years was over.

It must be said they were not people to pore over decisions. Having discretion over a great deal meant less to them, having never had much of it. A place on the earth to live was not a spiritual matter, but a practical one. His family were immigrants. He traveled for a living. Her family were backwoods itinerants. The two of them had kept the apartment on Center Street but rarely slept there. They had no great experience of *residence*. It might've been a small matter where they decided to go to have their baby. Me.

They thought first of New Orleans, where they liked it. It was not central, but life seemed possible there. Barney Rozier and Marie were in Gentilly — the suburbs—in a four-room, flat-roof, aqua-tinted stucco house with a tiny lawn. They had seen what that was, but chose against it. Jackson, Mississippi, was just up the road. They knew two people there, though not well. It must've seemed less exotic, more normal—which it was. It *was* the middle of where he drove to—Alabama, north Louisiana, south Arkansas. Plus, Jackson was nearer to Little Rock, and in a way like it. A small, southern capital. To be able to choose might've felt good. Grown-up—finally. They would be far enough away from everybody— his family and hers. Neither he nor she needed many people. Feeling *un*assimilated was no more unfamiliar than feeling assimilated.

In Jackson, then, they rented half a duplex, four small rooms including a bath, in the older central part of town. North Congress Street, down the hill from the capitol building. The flat came with an option to buy. There were old mansions up the street where legislators and hillbilly musicians took rooms, and where you could buy lunch or dinner. My mother was not a good cook, and they were used to eating out. There was a small yard front and back, a garage, neighbors, some older established houses where elderly widows peered out at you through the screens. These were already being converted to apartments. It was transitional. It was where you started if you came from someplace else.

I was born in the warm winter of 1944, in February, at the Baptist Hospital, at two A.M. I don't know if they cared that I would be a boy or a girl. But they were overjoyed—so they said—by me and by having made the commitment to live in Jackson and for their life to be altered in these ways. I don't know if my father was present for my birth. It was a Wednesday. He would normally have been on the road. Witnessing a birth wasn't *so* much a thing people did then. My mother's mother came down from Little Rock. None of his family chose to.

How would they work it all out—from an indistinct, undemanding future, to having a child, which is a very distinct future? She would now be what she had never been—a housewife-at-home alone, with

Edna, Richard, and Parker, Jackson, Mississippi, 1946

a child. A mother. She must've believed she was cut out for it. It was the more usual life. Things had been good up to now, and this might have seemed good, too—with the exception of my father's new absences.

For him, it would've been different, too. There was no single way to perform fatherhood—though he wouldn't have had those words. It wouldn't be good to be without her, having always *had* her—in the car with him, listening to her talk, enjoying her, eating with her, sleeping with her, letting himself be guided by what she thought and liked and wanted. Just *seeing* her. This was life he would miss. She *was* wide. He was less so. It had been all but perfect. Did he feel they were giving up something important? Was he ready for all of it? Probably he was, but no one asked the question in 1944. He would be gone now from Monday to Friday, even longer at the remoter reaches of his territory—Jackson, Tennessee. Far north Arkansas. Would he be lonely? Absolutely. Would she worry about other women, and he about other men slipping around? There had likely never been others for them. These thoughts might not have entered their minds.

But would it be permanent? *It*, meaning Jackson. The deep south. Mississippi, not Arkansas. No one knew.

And there was now me. Possibly I would not be the *only* baby. Did they think that? Did he or they wonder if I would grow up *different* without him there each and every day? If so, how? Would it be all right that "the father" was not a constant presence? How would he teach me things? Could a *presence* still be achieved? He himself had lacked a father, had grown up not being taught much. Did other boys have absent fathers? Could she compensate for him? Clearly, waiting for me to be born, they had just accepted how things would be. They loved each other and would love me. Love would be *presence* enough. We would be happy. And in that way—a way I think of as good, up to the very moment I write this—in that way my life began, and its lasting patterns became set.

STILL, THEY DID THEIR BEST to keep up the old ways—at least at the beginning. They took me.

The three of us in the hot car—in south Louisiana. Florence, Alabama. The Mississippi Delta. Bastrop, Shreveport. El Dorado and Camden, Arkansas. He now smoked El Productos, gained more weight—two-forty—wore better hats, went inside the whole-sale grocer houses to call on his accounts, leaving us outside in the front seat by the loading docks, in the heat or the cold. In New Orleans, my mother and I rode the Algiers Ferry back and forth while he worked as far as Houma and Lafayette. I crawled on the seawall at the lake, the wind whipping, the waves tufted. We went to City Park and Bayou St. John and Shell Beach, went to the zoo. We sometimes took the train—the "Miss Lou"—down from Jackson to Hammond just to meet him for a day. Once there was a car breakdown in Ville Platte, which took two weeks to fix. We waited there in a hot hotel room. Once there was a car breakdown on the high span of the river bridge at Greenville. My father was quick out into the feverish heat and damp wind, sweating in his shirtsleeves, changing the tire on the company Ford, high above the brown, sliding river, while inside my mother held me as tight as she could, as if I—the only child—might fly away.

I was not a bad baby, so it was almost thinkable to live this way—traveling with me across the south. But it couldn't last. Problems mounted. Hotel rooms, the places they'd always eaten, car problems. Predictable baby troubles. Finally, the decision they'd made before I was born, about the days he'd be away, the days we'd be at home—these would have to be honored.

And how was it for him? Driving, driving alone? Sitting in those hotel rooms, in lobbies, reading a strange newspaper in the poor lamplight; taking a walk down a street in the evening, smoking? Eating supper with some man he knew off the road? Listening to the radio in the sweep and hum of an oscillating fan. Then turning in early to the noise of katydids and switch-yards, car doors closing and voices on the street laughing into another night. How was it being a father *this* way—having a wife, renting a house in a town where they knew almost no one and had no friends, coming home only weekends, as if this *were* home?

It could only have been strange. Though possibly

Richard, Jackson, Mississippi, 1947

he might also have felt competent for the first time. Independent. Finally prepared for life. Approaching forty. A parent. He was not the kind of man to regret much or to take his temperature, or to look over his shoulder at what had once been different. Instead, he was the kind of man to know how he'd worked things out up to then, and to let that be. He knew he was mostly absent. He knew she was looking after their life and me, and that it was complex for her. He *was* a presence, if not a father precisely. And he was her husband, the man she loved and waited for. It was acceptable. And it was how their life would now go on—at least until his heart attack in 1948, the one he wouldn't die from, but the point at which everything changed again, when death and the fear of it became his familiars, and my mother's, too.

AN ONLY CHILD ABSORBS A GREAT DEAL—possibly more if his parents are older. An only child's imagination is strummed melodically by the things they say and don't say. I have always said and still believe my childhood was a blissful one. But that is not quite to say that life was normal. Their age wasn't normal for having a first child. Even in their view it wasn't. There was, unspoken, the sense that *they* should've been younger, or *I* should've been born fifteen years before, when they were new. I grew up feeling I should be older, or *was* older. There had already been so much important life *before* me—of which I knew little, and that to them did not bear talking about since it did not include me. I have no memory of either of them saying—as I grew older—"Richard, do you remember?" Or, "Richard, once, your father and I. . . ." What they talked about and what was in the air was only the *present*, interrupted by the long times between Monday and Friday. These absences made their closeness to each other even more paramount, since together was where they'd always, only been. I was where things had deviated and always sensed that. For all this to be a blissful life, love is certainly required, and a willingness—on my part—to fill some things in and deflect others.

His being gone must've created strains. My mother never complained in my hearing, though she was volatile—even in her loving. A shouter, a smacker, a frowner and a glowerer. Suddenly she'd had a baby. Suddenly she was too much alone in a strange city where old ties mattered and newcomers were foreigners. Possibly something about *me*—about my nature—also made things straitened. When I began to talk, I talked a great, great deal and wasn't naturally passive or compliant. When he was gone, life with her was never completely calm. Though when he was back, calm was instantly, rigorously enforced. Which created its own strains.

As time went on, did I ever sense that something was wrong between them? No. It was my child's outlook to think most things were *right*. And yet if life's eternal drama is of events seeking a more perfect state, their life and mine was not that. My recalled feelings over that time—my little-boy life, in Jackson, on Congress, in my first years, in the forties and beginning fifties—are of a hectic, changing, provisional existence. They loved me, protected me. But the experience of life was of *events,* of things and people in motion, and of being often alone and to the side of things. Which did not make me sorry and does not now. But life wasn't calm.

What did my father actually *think* about his situation, if he thought anything? Undoubtedly he thought, without much specificity, that there would be something more that would happen later. If he wondered whether he was good at fatherhood, he probably thought he was. He would've believed he was a good and pleasing pressure in the air of rooms he and we occupied; a continually welcome arrival into my mother's life and mine. He might've actually thought he was *not absent at all*, but present—only not in body: just not there for doctor visits, for the dentist, to take me to kindergarten at Mrs. Nelson's, to Sunday school; later on, for parent-teacher meetings, Cub Scouts, the swimming pool, the library, school pageants, and later yet for baseball try-outs and junior high graduation. This not-being-precisely-there is what was required to have his good job. And wasn't I always brought along—to visit their few friends, to be put into bedrooms to sleep while beyond the wall they were drinking and talking and laughing? And there was New Orleans again, the Gulf Coast, Pensacola, occasionally Atkins and Little Rock—the places they went. There would be time—the *later* that was to come—to teach me things, to impart onto me a way to be. He called me "son." I called him "Daddy." People said I looked like him. He would not have thought that seventy years later I cannot remember the sound of his voice, but long to.

And for me, how was it?

I could not have formulated the thought that when I was a young child growing up, he was then a younger husband undergoing the transformation to being an oldish father; or that what my mother was experiencing in herself and with me, he was experiencing the other side of. He was my father. I knew that was important. I knew his physical dimensions. There was his leaning-forward sweetness, his humor. His uncertainty-seeking-certainty. His bodily softness and rich smell. I knew the words for what he did to make a living. I knew the words for where he went—things I'd have known from infancy.

But did we have "interactions"? Of course. I must have told him about things—learning to swim at the YMCA, about General MacArthur's visit to Jackson in 1952, which he missed. About trying (unsuccessfully) to earn Cub Scout badges. And later, about wanting to go to Camp Mondamin. I have no memory of anything being a problem, of ever feeling I wasn't getting him enough. There was a way that his not being there most of the time became a kind of privileged state for me, a distinction among the other boys. It was as if I came to like having him gone. Though it also meant that I could not—when those same boys eventually asked—paint a clear picture of my life in one sentence or even four.

I have already said that what I don't know about my parents ought not be thought a quality of *their* lives. And yet, for me—different from my mother and different from him—his continual absence, much more than his intermittent presences, has become (and perhaps was all along through childhood) much of who he was. Memory has pushed him further and further away until I "see" him—in those early days—as a large, smiling man standing on the other side of a barrier made of air, looking at me, possibly looking *for* me, recognizing me as his son but never coming quite close enough for me to touch.

How we lived in Jackson was smally. My mother, who'd been taught by nuns, now joined the Presbyterians—a church close to our house—because my kindergarten teacher was a member there. "Accepted by profession of faith" my mother's certificate stated. My father, who never attended, joined "by letter," though he'd been raised a Presbyterian. A red-brick school—Jefferson Davis School—was next door, where it still sits. I was to go there. My mother was friendly—when she knew you—but did not make friends easily and was suspicious of the other children on our street, children who lived in rooming houses in upstairs apartments. Being a transient herself, she looked askance at transients. There were the old families in their big white houses up and down the block. They, in their turn, were wary of us. My mother and I ate in the boarding-houses up Congress by the capitol, two blocks south. Or sometimes we bought our meals at the steam-table at the grocery, which was not far away. We walked to town, the two of us—to the two department stores or to the movies. I rode the bus alone to kindergarten, walked the two blocks from the stop down Keener Ave, then took the bus home after lunch. Most always, he was not there—my father. Though I remember his Ford sitting at the curb on weekends, remember the sound of him in the house, in the bathroom, snoring in his bed. I remember the size of him. His leather suitcase was never unpacked. His change, wallet, pocket-knife, handkerchief, and watch were on his bed table (they did not sleep together anymore). The soapy smell of his shaving kit sweetened the bathroom. I can hear him singing—something about "the wig-a-zees and the bees in the trees," which made them both laugh, and sometimes he sang "Danny Boy." I hear the names repeated of the people he knew. Ole Mac. Lew Herring. Always, Mr. Hoyt up in KC. Mr. Beeham, Mr. Hoyt's boss. Kenny somebody.

Snapshots come into play. Tiny, square, scalloped black-and-whites. My mother bought a box Brownie and was bent to capture my father and me together: a bulky man in a dark overcoat, at first holding me, then "walking" me on the sidewalk in front of our house and the school yard; leaning over me in my toy car; later, me sitting in *his* car, smiling out the window wearing a baseball cap as if I'd just driven up. My mother's shadow lives in these, her perfect silhouette holding the camera at her waist, peering into it. Often lying in my bed at night, I heard the bed-springs squeeze—squeeze-squeeze, squeeze-squeeze—their low voices, encased in the old intimacy and in the anticipation of his regular departures—Monday gone, Friday returned.

What could I possibly have thought about my life? Most of it, of course, would've been just sensation, not thoughts, and much of *that* just anticipation. Of him. And once he was home again, anticipation that the week's events—its pleasures, displeasures, minor controversies, remonstrances, the complications my mother and I experienced—these would all be suspended or ignored. Or explained away quickly. It made for an atmosphere of agreed-upon concealment, of small dissemblings, of putting a good face on, of judging *this* to be more important than *that*, even when both mattered. These may have been the first of the lessons my father hoped to impart onto me, coping skills for issues that won't iron out yet need to be dealt with, and for which explanations must be available. If these were not the intended lessons, they were the ones I learned. My father's job was hard. He was delicate (probably he was by then). She would not risk distressing him. I was her ally, like it or not.

The grandparents played their part—at least *her* family did.

They were now established in Little Rock—Bennie and Essie. They ran a big hotel—the Marion. They had more money, more time. Ben Shelley kept blooded bird dogs in the hotel basement, drove a red Buick "Super." A four-holer. Was a sport. They came to Jackson at Christmas, or we went to them, bundled into my father's Ford with starch samples in the back, driving up through the Delta, across the river into Arkansas—five hours plus. We stayed in their big apartment in the hotel. #604. It was festive, jovial, boozy. They all still liked one another—an unusual family. There was a sense of re-uniting and resuming from the time before I was there. Plus I *was* there, included now. It was the happiest life I'd known.

In these joint festivities, my father was a son-in-

Bennie, Richard, and Essie, Hot Springs, Arkansas, 1954

law again—but a father, too. Older. Though now he was 5th—since I was there and much was made of me. Bennie was a boisterous, fat, rakish, pugnacious, sharp-eyed capable man everyone liked, and who cut a swath. A lesser, slightly ludicrous public personage in Little Rock, with his name frequently in the papers. Whereas my father—tall, fleshy, slightly shy, understated but willing, and with the politeness of a more modest-size man—was still a country boy who'd made it to where he'd made it but wasn't going much further. He stood aside for my grandfather, who captivated me. My father was part of an audience and seemed not to mind.

His brother still lived in town. "Uncle Pat" was heavy, grim-faced, sullen, with a tiny wife crippled by arthritis. Aunt Nora. He booked circus acts for the state fair and had little to say. Terrible things he'd seen in the war were the ostensible reason for his silence. They had no children. On these holiday trips we saw him only in his small house on South Spring Street, and never for longer than an hour. I did not have a brother, so how they were together became the way brothers were. Not close.

On Christmas morning, we always drove to Atkins, to his mother's, two hours west. We ate Christmas dinner with the likable cousins and his sister
and her unlikable pharmacist husband. My father
watched his mother stump around her house in fer-
vid insistence that things weren't the way they were.
Dislike or distrust or just dismay with my mother underlay this. Everyone acted polite. I was pronounced
to look more like an Uncle William—a deceased
Irishman. My father was doted on, teased. Everyone
half wished he would stay longer. But we did not. A
day was all.

Following which, it was the long, wintry drive
back to Jackson and to how events went on there—
the leaving and the coming, my father's appearance
on the weekends; my mother and me alone in the
little brick house with the sycamore in front. If I
could've asked them, they might've said these were
also exquisite times. They were in their forties—the
clear-horizon years, when if you had a better idea you
could give it a try. Have another child. Find a better
job. Buy a new car. Buy the duplex on Congress—
which they did. Mississippi was alien, costive, but

it was just a small, ignorable part of the whole. My mother didn't have to work. We had a maid to clean and look after me when she went to the library or to a movie or shopping. She bought a piano so I could someday take lessons. When he was home there was time for picnics at Pelahatchie Lake, for day trips to the Confederate bluffs at Vicksburg, to Stafford Springs to swim, to Allison's Wells, to Jack's tamale house, to the bootlegger across the river, to the airport to watch planes take off. I don't know how other people saw them, or if my life—loved, looked after, cloistered by my parents' circumstances and personalities—was like other boys' lives. Again, I don't remember my mother complaining about anything. But for myself, I must've been beginning to sense that his being gone was not the exception, but the ordinary, identifying dimension of everything. People go away. Possibly I was becoming more aware of my father as someone *not* there, and less aware of him in the days and moments he was actually present. Permanence became something you fashioned. This may have been another lesson he imparted to me.

I DON'T REMEMBER THE TIME OF YEAR of his heart attack—the first one. Something makes me think it was in spring, because when the ambulance came to our house in the middle of the night—the men with a stretcher walking right down the hall—they took him out the front door, and I don't remember it being cold or hot. I remember only being confused and alarmed, since nothing like this had ever happened in the comings and goings that made up our life.

Everything changed on that night, of course. Remembered time can shift and wander. But I was definitely four. I knew something about absence but I knew nothing about change. I knew nothing about my father's heart, or about what my mother felt: her husband, aged forty-three, in the Baptist Hospital—where I'd been born—laid out under an oxygen tent, not breathing well. Both of them so young.

We went to the hospital, she and I. Possibly it was later that same morning. I saw him under his big, clear tent—as big as a pup tent. We would say today that he was *stabilized*, but I didn't know what had happened—what he'd suffered, how it had felt. I heard the words—*heart attack*. But he was strangely smiling out at me through the plastic, as if this was just a very funny situation to find yourself in. Possibly he didn't want me to be afraid, though I wasn't. He was large under the sheets, but didn't look sick. He was breathing normally, it seemed to me. His doctor, Dr. Hageman, must've told my mother and him many things (I of course wasn't told anything): that Parker could be fine; though also that his life could now be shortened; that he should lose weight, work less, not smoke, take exercise, not drink, find a hobby, possibly even should put his affairs in order. People knew less about heart attacks then. But no one took it lightly. And while I could not have said so, I must have sensed, just from being present beside them, that wherever life had seemed to be going *before*, it might be going there differently now. Or it might be going somewhere else. Here was change. His mother did not come down from Atkins to see him, though Bennie and Essie did.

It's tempting, as I sit here sixty-eight years later, to focus a shadowy, melodramatic light on my father's remaining life; to see it as *the time between his heart attack and before he would suddenly die.* This would be accurate, since that is what that time was. Again, Dr. Hageman would've told him what was wrong—the heart murmur—and about how things could go; that the time ahead was unassured. Death was a likelihood, but nothing more was ordained. He was alive now. These things he knew. And yet it is also true that this period, between 1948 and 1960, encompasses the entire time—I can say it now—that I knew my father not just as *a* father or *the* father, but was the only time and the only terms under which I fully realized I *had* a father. To write a memoir and to consider the importance of another human being is to try to credit what might otherwise go unremarked—partly by acknowledging that mysteries lie within us all, and by identifying within those mysteries, virtues. Once more, it's not so different from what we find when we read a story by Chekhov, nor is it probably very different from the problem any son faces when thinking about and estimating his parents. The *truest* life, of course, is always the life that's lived. But how I, his only child, can best credit and characterize my father's life and its virtues is as he lived it in my gaze, which is to say, without the overlay of later, unhappy knowledge, life lived as if there would always be a tomorrow, right to the moment when there was not.

So THEN, THE LAST TWELVE YEARS of my father's earthly life. It is little easier than the early parts to make clear, since he was, again, not there with us much. What I remember of him between my ages five and sixteen, in fact, stands away from time like islands in the horizon-to-horizon sea of his absence. Things that took place when I was nine mingle uncertainly with what happened when I was twelve and fourteen. And if his absence had for a time become a kind of presence, it now became less that, as my own life crowded in with its concerns. Somehow in these years there seems to be less of him even when there was more.

HE RECOVERED—at least in a way he did. There was no surgery, then, for what he had. He was given no pills to take. There would be convalescence—some taking it easy. But from my standpoint, he was in the hospital, and then he just resumed life.

He did set aside cigarettes, though he did not take any exercise. Driving his territory was deemed stressful, and since I was not in school yet, my mother and I rode with him once again, with her now driving. When having me along—age four—became impractical, I was sent to Little Rock to live with the grandparents in the Marion. How long this went on, I don't know. A year, possibly, with me back and forth to Arkansas; while the two of them did what they'd done before I was born. Lived on the road while he recovered and got stronger. They might've loved it.

My age, of course, soon changed that arrangement. Kindergarten and then school. Her helping with the driving was now confined to summer. To stay off cigarettes, he opportunistically affected a pipe, which was thought to be better. He gained weight. He developed hemorrhoids and big corns on both his feet (which he carved away at with a safety razor blade, while seated on the bedside when he was home, and as I watched). He now limped—

possibly from the corns. His affect became *burdened*. His breath was shorter and he wheezed. He lost hair. Something inimical and sinister in the way the company Fords were made—a flaw in the design of the door-front moldings—caused him more than once to close the car door on his hand, wounding him but not breaking a bone. It was before the days of lawsuits for such things. He tried to be more careful. But overall he was weakened.

In Kansas City his bosses contemplated his situation and relaxed his duties, divided his territory into two parts and gave one to Dee Walker. My mother attended him as lavishly as possible. And yet, he very well might've felt trapped—trapped inside his defective body, trapped in a now-stressful job he'd always loved, trapped in his car and in all those tiny hotel rooms and coffee shops, trapped as the father of a son he saw only on weekends—when he came home exhausted, needing calm and sympathy and sleep. He might also have felt remote from his only love, whose affections and time she was now required to share with me. He also might simply have hurt and been scared.

I do not know about my father's faith—if he
had any. He might've said he did—after his heart
attack. But he did not practice one, not as long as I
knew him. I know he didn't take pleasure in books—
where he could've found what we all find if we don't
have faith: testimony that there is an alternate way
to think about life, different from the ways we're
naturally equipped. Seeking imaginative alternatives
would not have been his habit.

Like any of us he certainly possessed an ongoing,
interior narrative, yet he was not notably inward. He
was also not of a complaining nature. It was not natural for him to think life was inadequate or required
much bettering, or of himself as singular or standing out for special notice. He lacked obvious hubris
or great ambitions and fitted himself better than
most into daily existence—even now when his had
grown uncertain. In most ways, he was a man who
took life as it randomly came, and was good at avoid-
ing what he didn't want to think about. Being sick.
These native qualities that maybe bottled him up as
an uneducated country boy may also have defended
him. And as time went on he may have thought that

his doctors would save him, and wished to portray himself as strong for my mother. But he would also have known that even though he could be approaching death, nothing in her love for him would change. He was in most ways not a dexterous or skillful man, but in the art of being loved he possessed a talent— which surely is a virtue worth noting, one that confers benefits superior to most.

I MYSELF DO NOT REMEMBER thinking much about my father being ill. Only that he *had* been ill but was mostly all right now. Twice, I recall, he had bursitis and stayed off the road, in bed for a week. And there were the times when he shut his hand in the company-car door. But his heart was never talked about in my hearing. The signal life events of this period were not, at least in my understanding, health related.

Did *he* fear death and think about it? Probably both. Did he experience tension and worry because of it? I'm certain. But was he an even more partial father than when I was younger? Not that I recall.

I remember being aware that my relation to him seemed different from what I observed were other boys' relations to their fathers. I was aware of no one whose father was a traveling salesman and always gone. (There of course may have been several.) Other fathers seemed to go to banks or be pharmacists or work in the oil & gas business or own car dealerships or construction firms or pest controls. Though it would be inaccurate to say I felt loss arising from this difference. To my view, we were not a determinedly unusual family. Not poor. Not rich. Close-knit, though shying away—by instinct and mostly without choice   from full entry to the life of Jackson. I grew up understanding that the view from outside any family, mine included, and the experience of being inside would always be different.

From other photographs of him through these years, I think I "see" in my father's soft, willing features—and photographs always bear the imprint of the viewer's later knowledge and needs—a hesitancy, a lack of wryness, a hint of reluctance and frustration, a faint awareness of some sort of impendment. How would that not be true? And yet, we went on traveling back and forth to Arkansas—where I was again often left with my grandparents in their big hotel and was happy. Other times, with my mother along, we made holidays out of his trade shows. We drove to Kansas City, took short outings to the Coast and back, and as always to New Orleans. Sometimes in summers I rode alone in the car with him, to Louisiana or to Alabama, while my mother stayed home and rested. We slept together—we must've—in the same steamy hotel-room beds where they had slept, ate in the same three-dollar restaurants. I sat in the car, as she had, and waited while he called on his small-town customers. During these trips my father and I treated each other with unaccountable correctness and courtesy. Away from my mother's oversight and occasional volatility, a new and possibly natural decorum took over. Nothing of their life-on-the-road before I came was rehearsed to me. Nothing regarding his current situation was complained about or even mentioned. My view about anything was seldom sought. If his life during this time was straitened by poor health or worry, his mantra (and of course he didn't have a mantra) was that all was normal.

During the regular weeks when he was gone, my mother and I simply carried on. And on the weekends, his convenience (serenity, meals-on-time, extra sleeping, taking drives into the countryside) commanded almost all discretion and activity. Together, the two of them must now have lived in an even more intense *present,* made intenser by my being there, by their being so close to one another, by their being unaffiliated in Jackson, and by my father's un-discussed *condition.* This undoubtedly is how all families operate, or would. But, if I say that when I was growing up my father's life was headed in one direction and mine in another, I can also say that I was never aware of it, never thought of myself as being disadvantaged or kept in the dark. I was their son. I trusted them.

Which is not to say there was never tension or disruption at ground level. My father's temper now became a feature I learned about firsthand. A man can be courteous, affable, and shy but still have furies. And my father's furies doubtless flamed from the silent dysfunctions of his heart and a maddening sense of frailty. Possibly, too, he was depressed—but wouldn't have known that word. He practiced no hobbies or sports, entertained no committed interests or enthusiasms apart from work and us. He was impulsive and not adept at most endeavors requiring patience, and would quickly lose his temper. He could not make a TV work when he wanted it to, which suddenly would infuriate him. He could not reliably start a power lawn mower, which also infuriated him. He could not properly hang a punching bag in the utility room of the suburban house we eventually moved into. (It fell at the first blow.) He tried to paint by numbers as a form of relaxation, but did not finish his portrait of a golden palomino. He could not erect a basketball backboard so that when I got older I could gain a place on the school team. He could not operate a rotary barbecue or string up a hammock. When he half-reluctantly took me to dingy pay-to-fish lakes in the Delta—Bee Lake—or onto crowded, sweltering "deep-sea" excursions into the Gulf, neither of us caught anything, and both grew sullen, and in his case ill-tempered. He'd rather have been home with my mother.

Once we went to the Natchez Trace to cut a Christmas tree—illegally. He wanted a small tree;

I wanted a large one, and prevailed. But when we brought the tree inside the house and could not fit it into our low-ceilinged living room, my own temper went off. I dragged the tree outside to shorten its trunk with a handsaw. My father came behind me in a fit of anger all his own. He took the saw away, snatched up the Christmas tree and cut it off *at the top*—thereby, in my view, maiming it. I then grabbed the mangled tree back and, as well as I could, *threw it at him*. Whereupon he gave me a whipping I do not now want to think too much about because of its sudden-ness and ferocity. There weren't many such events, but this was not the only one.

I cannot remember, over the years, my father ever explicitly teaching me much—except to ride a bicycle, and how the column shifter worked on his 3-speed Ford coupé. He did not teach me to read and did not, that I remember, ever read *to* me. He did not teach me to tie knots or to hunt or to shoot a gun or how to start a campfire or how to change a spark plug or a tire. He may have tried to teach me how to bait a hook, but it may have been not the correct way, since it never worked out that a fish was caught. He did not take me to movies or to the swimming pool. He didn't talk to me about sex or girls, about religion, about his own worries, about current events or politics—other than that he and my mother had liked Roosevelt, though he never said why. I don't know what he thought about racial matters or about what I should grow up to be someday (when of course he wouldn't be there). I do not recall ever having an actual *discussion* with him; I don't remember him asking me what was going on in my mind. When we walked down a street side-by-side—to the post office to mail off his expense reports on Sunday mornings, or when we were in the car, driving his sales route—I cannot imagine what we said. School for me was far from easy, but he never—to my memory—asked me about my grades or what subjects I liked. These were my mother's concerns, he must've thought. In all of these goings and comings performed together, of course things were said, passing life was observed, feelings voiced, views and amusements shared. Necessarily they would. But these are lost to time now and to superceding events. I wish I could remember them, if only because not remembering them portrays our life in a way it wasn't, makes him and me together seem to be lonely and remote from each other in a way I honestly believe we weren't. When I think about my father through the haze of all these poorly recollected details, my truest and most affectionate assessment of him was that he was not a *modern* father. Indeed, even then, when I knew him best, he seemed to be from another place and another time far away.

Still. He accompanied me and my mother to the Baptist Hospital when I was eight and had my tonsils and adenoids out on the same day. Once he patiently doctored me with a menthol inhaler when I had asthma—though the inhaler suddenly malfunctioned and sprayed hot water in my face. Which made him cry. He bought me more than one dog and at least three cats, one of which my mother backed over in the driveway. There were several Easter chicks, two ducks and two rabbits, all of which subsequently vanished. He, once in a while, took me to a high school football game—though we knew no one playing and always left early. He bought me a baseball glove (a cheap one), and now and then would play catch in the back yard—though he was not good at that and never did it for long or seemed to enjoy it. Once, when I played especially poorly on my Babe Ruth League team, it happened to be on a rare night when he came. In the dark car on the way home, he seemed disappointed and told me I needed to play better but then said it was all right. Later, when I was in junior high, he would regularly drive me to school on his way out of town on Mondays, but was never there on other days.

As I record these events, I realize that like many renditions of childhood, mine—under time's ruthlessness—might seem incomplete or lacking. I do not believe, however, that I was ever ignored or given a short straw, or that my father was anything but a good father—as good as he could be. I could not have said it at the time, but an unspoken part of my awareness must've been that I was the only son of a man who was trying to conduct life against odds. I can only intuit what was his *effect* on me. But if I had to I would say that because I was his son, I can recognize now that life is short and has inadequacies, that once again it requires crucial avoidances as well

Parker, Edna, and Richard, Biloxi, Mississippi, 1957

as fillings-in to be acceptable. Most everything but love goes away.

So then, at a time when I might've been expected to notice and remember more, my father's absence from home became increasingly an unremarked *given*, something I could work with, dream up a private life around and make the most of.

Officially—in my mother's view—I needed now to be more under my father's influence. I was disruptive and undisciplined in school. I read poorly. I continued to talk too much. I didn't study, came home with poor grades, and was secretive, willful and unpredictable by age ten—all qualities that could be typical of a boy with undiagnosed learning difficulties and a largely absent father. A firmer hand might've been useful.

And yet, although I was nominally expected to operate more and more in his field of notice, he was still almost always gone, so that I had little awareness of how he or I fitted into this new, more urgently formative stage of my life. We were both growing older, but for me there was no sensation of our *becoming* anything together. In spite of what was expected, he remained a *weight*—like gravity—that I felt from off to the side of things. A force largely unseen.

When he came home weekends, life was neither worse nor better. Our house was simply less large with him in it. His and my associations were frequent but fitful, his weight upon me not persistent. Things surfaced, then went under again. He was not a stranger, but he was *like* a stranger, and while it was foregone that he loved me, it's possible he looked upon me the way I looked upon him. I have sometimes thought over these years that I had my father at a time in a boy's life when having a father did not mean so much. But that is the opposite of true, and would only seem true to a boy whose father was mostly not there.

But how *he* felt and how he experienced life is what matters here, and mattered to my mother and me. The twelve years between his first heart attack and his dying, the time of my late childhood and mid-adolescence, was his *only* life, all he had left, the time when he was as much himself as he would ever be again. I should step back from events as much as I can.

I don't remember him being unhappy. As I said, he was never an unhappy man. Though our particular version of father and son was not leisurely or capacious, and he seemed fidgety when he was home, as if seeking comfort but not quite finding it. He grew to have a belly and lost even more hair, but he stayed mannishly handsome, and the two of them—my parents—remained an attractive couple. When I see his face in pictures from this time—the mid-fifties now—he looks mildly impatient, as if trying to feel relaxed. He limped and did not stand up especially straight. Though there were no new heart crises, no worsening of whatever his condition was—nothing I was told about. I had all but forgotten his heart attack.

What pleasure he took in me, in having a son, I cannot say—only that he did not seem to take none. His temper tended to flare, often with me as its natural focal point, given my behavior. There was the matter of the Christmas tree. I subsequently cut down some *other* trees on a neighbor's property. I was building "a fort." We were in the suburbs by then. This infraction ignited him, and he whipped me hard. He and my mother experienced their own upsets—sometimes with me present. Occasionally they shouted. Drinking was usually involved. One night on St. Louis Street in New Orleans he held her against a brick building wall late at night, after we'd eaten at Antoine's. They were shouting. No disputes, however, carried over even to the next day. It wasn't that they didn't get along. This was just the *way* they got along. And all was over fast because they *did*.

But I became watchful—of him, as if he was more unpredictable than he was. I kept him at more of a distance from things I did and said. Possibly it's what any teenage boy does with his father. I did not confide in him, which—because I was secretive—wasn't my habit in general. I did not ask him for much—pocket change, use of the car when I passed fifteen, permission to buy a motorcycle, permission to take a paper route—all granted. As I've said, I did not do well in school, but he didn't seem to take an active interest or express concerns. Conceivably he had not been good at school and knew there were paths in life that didn't involve school or great accomplishment. Selling starch. Following in his footsteps. This, we never discussed.

Who clearly was the center of his life was my mother. To her, I might've been becoming more a center—with a damaged husband who might not live long. But to him it was her. Even at the time, I knew I was third. Which was ideal, since I could watch them, overhear them through doors, listen to the bed-springs at night when he came from his room to visit hers—all without attracting much notice to myself. Their being so much a "unit" freed me and became another luxury, born of how life was being constructed.

When he came home on Friday nights, bringing his packages from wherever he'd been, it was to find her. When he laughed (and he often did), it was because of something she'd said. When he didn't understand something (which was frequent, too), she would make it clear. When the in-laws came at Christmas, or we went to them in Little Rock, he watched her. When we went to his mother's in Atkins, he sat or stood near to my mother. He was her protector, but she was his. If it meant that I was further from the middle of things, I have lived my entire life thinking this is the proper way to be a family.

AT SOME POINT, near the time I was ten, in 1954, I became aware that my father had begun to crave the suburbs, and simultaneously to crave a new car—something better than the company Ford—two new things that would be his and his alone. Some rich aspect of life must've suddenly seemed within his reach, or urgently just outside it. He wanted these desires met, as if he was in a hurry.

New cars began appearing in our driveway on Congress Street. These were *demonstrators*—a term of sales art now lost. Spanking new two-tone Dodges arrived with fins and big mirrored bumpers and whipping antennas. Shiny Bel Airs. Much nicer Fords. A chromed-up Pontiac Star Chief worth twenty-six hundred. Young, skinny, crew-cut salesmen delivered these to us for weekend try-outs, most of which time the cars sat out front for the neighbors to see—briefly presumed to be ours. My father would stand on our tiny lawn, smoking his pipe, considering the cars carefully, or he would muse at them out the bedroom window, presumably making up his mind. Then on Monday they'd go back. He and my mother had decided, though no one had told me how.

But on Saturday afternoons and after church on Sunday, we would all three pile in the new car (not to be ours) and take a test drive north of the city, into the new, spreading, suburban outskirts where my father dreamed we would soon be moving. Meadowbrook, Northside, Hanging Moss, Sherwood Forest, Watkins Drive. Cul-de-sacs. Haphazardly lined-out developers' tracts. Many of these subdivisions-to-be were only farmers' fields or pine scrubbage dropping off into the Pearl River swamp, where deer and bobcats and turkeys abided, but where soon would be streets and houses and schools. Buyers could choose a lot or a half-built *spec* house or a finished model home with furniture already inside. Close-by, the Interstate was creeping north. Land would soon be filled in clear to Chicago.

Specifically what was the character of my father's longing—as we motored slowly in those fancy *demos*, down one curving, unfinished street and up another, weekend upon weekend, time when I might've been doing something else but was required to be with them, as my father trained his gaze hungrily out at the passing houses, as if glimpsing a bright fantasy in the clouds—I don't know.

Once, late on a shady Sunday, we found our way down such a gravel trace, an old lovers' lane where a hand-lettered sign said LOTS. At the end we came upon police cars. Some boy had killed his girlfriend in the woods there, then killed himself. A uniformed patrolman walked up to our borrowed car, leaned into the window, shaking his head, his hat off. "Oh, folks, you don't want to see what's down there," he said, "I promise you that." We backed around and drove slowly home, as though our search had reached the place where civilization ended.

It's likely, of course, that nothing was unusual about this new yearning my father had fallen under. Almost certainly he felt his days were fewer than they had been, and might've fastened down on the thought of a new house and a fancy car with the zeal of just such a man—re-investing in the world, as if a promise of more life for the three of us came with that bargain. It's also just as possible to think of him—for once—as a man of his time. If the suburbs were *not* his glimpsed dream in the clouds, they were nonetheless there and new, and he could go toward them—a country boy with no wish to return to the country, who'd exceeded his station and found himself free to think of things many other people thought of.

I, of course, had come to like where we lived on Congress. I had friends—a few. I had adapted to the inevitability of school. I lacked my father's sense of impendment, so that my world worked on relatively simple principles. You lived where you lived, knew who you knew. When my parents discussed moving, when they spent evenings at the dining room table totaling and re-totaling their finances, working out a strategy for enrolling me in a newer, "better" school, of moving us away from neighbors they knew toward neighbors they didn't, it was never discussed with me. There were the Sunday drives, the houses. But I didn't take any of that too seriously. They didn't seem to be people who would change life drastically once it had found its place—as it had. Even now they do not seem

that way. And so once again I approach their other-
ness and they elude me, as our parents do.

There were a few close calls, inching my father
nearer the purchase of a house. An offer was hesi-
tantly extended to a Mr. Culley, but was declined and
some ill will generated in my father. Another time he
acquired some basic blueprints you could send off for
from *Town and Country* magazine. Numerous conversations were conducted with builders—large men in
khakis and white shirts—my father standing beside
them in the middle of some half-finished street, holding his rolled-up plans and pointing toward a parcel
where a home could go up. There was one finished
house he liked enormously but failed to qualify for
at the bank. He became more intent and impatient,
but was too courteous, too stand-offish, too lacking
in knowingness—even with my mother's aid—to
drive home a bargain.

Time passed. Possibly he dreamed at night with
greater vividness of me mowing a lawn while he
watched. Of winding curb-less streets without transients for neighbors, of a yellow school bus stopping
and picking me up, of coming home on weekends to a

new house, of being viewed by new congenial neighbors, of the way my mother would look when she stood in the doorway each time he arrived on Friday. Smiling.

Between them, there began to be more audible talk about my "needing" to go to a better school. What was wrong with the one where I already went wasn't explained. There was also overheard comments about keeping the house on Congress as a rental, pocketing income and accruing equity. There was even talk of my mother's parents "helping out." My father's salary at Faultless had risen only to two seventy-five a month. There was a sensation of mounting—what? Tension? Anticipation? Need?

And then, one day, they suddenly bought a house—or my father did. Just one day, so it seemed to me. I had never seen it before, though it was on a street where we often drove slowly along. Berlin Drive. Number 4262.

The house was new and painted pale green—like the ones in Gentilly—with a water oak in the yard, a carport, three bedrooms, a red front door. It sat on a half-acre lot (it's still there today). Young neighbors were living next door at 4276—the Barfields, who *were* congenial. On the other side was an open field. Nearby streets were named after famous cities in Europe. Athens, Brussels, London—all Drives. In due time all would be a neighborhood. A Mr. Charles Galloway was the builder. Exact replicas of our house were on other streets nearby, in different colors. One had its carport on the other side. To me, these duplications were both strange and disappointing. Though if my father noticed them, he didn't talk about it.

My mother's parents came forward, as promised. My father lacked a sufficient *down*— $1,700—ten percent of the seventeen thousand asking price, much less than the cost of a used Ford today. A loan was arranged. He would manage the monthly payments. They would keep the house on Congress. Possibly this money from his in-laws was embarrassing, a diminishment. But no one said so. In short order, an Oldsmobile '88 was also purchased, new off the showroom floor—with what money I don't know. It had a pink top with a charcoal gray body—a color combination popular at the time.

I have singled out our new house and our shiny car because together they compose the last celebratable events of my intact family life. It's possible to believe that my two parents were already out on some long causeway of uncertainty, and that my father was trying to make this final *present* last. The suburbs gave him a sense of accomplishment, of affiliation, of having achieved both distance from where he'd begun, as well as some blessed distraction from his health troubles—all evidence that he had not failed. In other words, progress. Mississippi—up to now bland and indifferent—had become a place where he was a man of his own created circumstances. He was invisible, but different from how he'd *been* invisible. It satisfied him almost completely.

ONCE WE WERE THERE and settled on Berlin Drive, and I had started in the new school (where I not surprisingly hated it), and he had begun going to work again—gone Monday, home Friday—family life became surprisingly less manifest. The suburbs must facilitate this. I know my father was happy.

His good humor surged. He told jokes again and did some singing—though he did not become more relaxed. Photos again bear this out. He was liked by our new neighbors—they both were—although it was understood he would not be home much, and I to a degree would become a *de facto* charge of the neighborhood.

To me, he grew more marginal, even less a presence, more a shadow than a weight. This might've been the expected "later" time when he would teach me things, when we would grow close. But that did not happen, though again I can't say I felt deprived.

He had a concrete patio laid in, bought a new hammock, and an air conditioner for his company car. He became interested in planting pine trees behind the house—though he planted too many, too close together, and they didn't thrive. He set out tomato plants. He planted St. Augustine and azaleas and a magnolia tree—the state tree. Though once this new life was underway, he became broodingly concerned about his mother, in Atkins. She was in her eighties and declining. He feared she would soon die. So he drove the long distance back and forth to

Parker, Jackson, Mississippi, 1956

see her when he could. He attended more baseball games I played in, he drove his new car on the weekends, and once when I fell into trouble with the police for stealing car parts, he exhibited an unexpected patience and grace toward me, which my mother did not exhibit.

Did he now think about different things he could do apart from traveling and being away from us? He was not even fifty-five. Did the two of them, newly situated, consider new plans? Did they talk about all that time when it had just been the two of them along, and how far they'd come? I don't know. So much of the way I saw our life presumed continuity and the certainty of my own endurance. Knowing my parents' qualms, fears, their new longings in any way similar to the way I knew my own would be only approximate, given that they said almost nothing about such things. Conceivably it was a rich time for them together. Although it's likeliest that their thoughts about their future were merely that it would happen.

Which is what it did.

In retrospect, the advent of death can cast a too dramatic light on the events leading toward it.

As I said, he had not been sick, that I knew of. There had been no crisis of some other kind. My trouble with the police might've worried him. But since he'd been sympathetic about this, I'd begun to think he and I might inch closer now. My sixteenth birthday was soon to come, February 16th, 1960. He'd bought me a basic Gibson guitar, which I badly wanted, and had paid for some lessons. He and my mother were cheerful. He'd gone to the Senior Bowl football game in Alabama not long before—had gone by himself because he felt like it—and been pleased to be able. It was as if some new *breadth* in life had opened for him.

On a Friday night he came home as usual. It always seemed like he came from Louisiana. There was the usual elation in our new house. Bright lights. Some drinking in the kitchen, laughing, his jokes, rehearsing the week that'd ended. My mother made beef stroganoff—a new dish. Nothing was out of the ordinary. I watched *Rawhide* on TV. They went into her bedroom and closed the door. At some point later he went to bed, and then I watched television until midnight. And then I went to sleep.

At six I was awakened by my mother saying my father's name. "Carrol." Which is what she called him. "Wake up. Carrol. Wake up. What's the matter? Wake up." Then more loudly. "Wake up!"

I got out of bed in my pajamas, went into the hall and to the door of the next room, which was his. My mother was leaning forward beside his bed, over him. My father was gasping for air in his bed. His eyes were closed. He wasn't moving except for the gasps. He looked—his skin did—gray. "Wake up!" my mother said insistently but different from that. "Carrol, wake up." She held his shoulders, put her face close to his and shook him. But he did not move. "Richard, what's wrong with him?" she said. She looked around at me. She was about to cry and was becoming panicked. She was on the verge of something bad. It was February 20th, 1960—four days after my birthday.

I don't know if I said "I don't know" to her question. But I came forward, got up onto the bed where he was, and took both my father's shoulders in my hands and shook him. Very hard. Not as hard as I could, but hard. I said his name—Daddy—

several times. He took a deep breath in and let it out strenuously—in a way that made his lips flutter, as if he was trying to breathe (though I think he was dead). With my two hands, I turned his face upward, used my thumbs to pry his loose, fleshy mouth and teeth open, and I put my own mouth over his and breathed down into him, into his mouth and throat and (I imagined) into his chest. I didn't know how to do this, or if it made sense. I'd only heard about people doing it. But I did it several times, possibly ten. And the result of my efforts to breathe for him, or to bring my breath *to* him and wake him up and be alive, was nothing. He did not breathe again or utter another sound.

After some time on my knees, on his bed with him—when I must've begun to conceive the thought that he was dead—I got down and turned to my mother, who had by then backed into the open doorway and put her fists to her temples, watching all that was going on in front of her. I don't know that I said anything to her. I may have stifled some sound deep in myself. But my mother said, "Oh, no. Oh, no, no, no, no, no, no, no." Which is when I went past her—as she was saying this—and down the hallway to call the doctor. His house was not far from ours. Such things—the doctor coming—were more usual then than they are today.

THE REST IS TELL-ABLE BUT, TO ME, of less importance. My father, who died on that day, is buried in Atkins, Arkansas—not beside his wife but beside his mother and father. When my father was lying in the funeral home in Jackson and had been "viewed" for a day, his brother, Pat, came down from Little Rock, asked no one's permission, and quietly ordered my father's body to be transported on a freight car to Atkins for burial in a family plot too small for my mother to share. My mother, who was unhinged, heard about this only in the hours after the train had departed. It was too much for her, and too late to try to change anything—or so she felt. I was too young to be of use. My father's mother, Minnie, was still alive—eighty-three, born in County Cavan. This was how they did things. His mother would own him at the last.

Grievous wrong lives on in this act. And nothing's to be done. In the end, he was gone from my mother one last time. Right or wrong, in her way of thinking eternity would not be theirs together. It is not the saddest thing I know. But it is one of them. Out of respect for them, and out of love, I do not visit their two graves, since it was together that they knew life most brightly, and together I prefer to think of them.

But hardly an hour goes by on any day that I do not think *something* about my father. Much of these things I've written here. Some men have their fathers all their lives, grow up and become men within their fathers' orbit and sight. My father did not experience this. And I can imagine such a life, but *only* imagine it. The novelist Michael Ondaatje wrote about his father that ". . . my loss was that I never spoke to him as an adult." Mine is the same—and also different—inasmuch as had my father lived beyond his appointed time, I would likely never have written anything, so extensive would his influence over me have soon become. And while not to have written anything would be a bearable loss—we must all make the most of the

lives we find—there would, however, not now be
this slender record of my father, of his otherwise invisible joys and travails and of his virtue—qualities
that merit notice in us all. For his son, not to have left
this record would be a sad loss indeed.

My Mother, In Memory

Edna Akin, 1928

My mother's name was Edna Akin, and she was born in 1910, in the far northwest corner of Arkansas—Benton County—in a place the location of which I'm not sure of and never have been. Near Decatur or Centerton. A town that may no longer exist. Or not a town at all—just a rural place. That is near the Oklahoma border there, and in 1910 it was a rough country with a frontier feel. Only ten years before, robbers and outlaws had been loose on the landscape. Bat Masterson was still alive then and not long gone from Galena.

I remark on this not because of its susceptibility

to romance, or because I think it makes my mother's life unique, but because it seems like such a long time ago now, and such a far-off and unknowable place; and because it is my mother, whom I knew very well, who links me to that foreignness, that other thing I don't know much about and never did. This is one quality of our lives with our parents that is often overlooked, and so devalued. Our parents intimately link us, closeted as we are in our lives, to a thing we're not, forging a joined separateness and a useful mystery, so that even together with them we are also alone.

The act of considering my mother's life is an act of love. And my incomplete memory of her life should not be thought of as incomplete love. I loved my mother the way a happy child does, thoughtlessly and without doubts. And when I became an adult, and we were adults who knew one another, we regarded each other highly. We could always say "I love you" to clarify our complicated dealings without pausing. That seems perfect to me now and did then.

I have already said that my mother and my father were not a pair for whom history had much to offer. This might've had to do with not being rich or with their both being country people and insufficiently educated, or with not being particularly aware of many things. For my mother, history was just small business, forgettable residues—some of them mean. Nothing in her past was heroic or edifying. The Depression—hard times all around—had something to do with that. In the thirties, after they were married, they lived simply and only for each other and for the day. They drank some, lived on the road with my father's salesman's job. They had a good time and felt they had little to look back on, and didn't look.

About my mother's early life I don't know much—for instance, where *her* father came from. Akin suggests the possibility of Irish Protestants. He was a carter, and my mother spoke of him lovingly, though not at length. "Oh," she would say, "my daddy was a good man." And that was that. He died of cancer in the 1930s—but not before my mother had been relegated to him by *her* mother— almost a waif. This was before she was twelve. My sense is that they resided, daughter and father, back in the deep Ozark country, near where she was born, and that for her it had been a good time while it lasted. I don't know, however, how long that was, or what she was enthusiastic about when she was a young girl, or what her thoughts and hopes were. She never told me.

Of *her* mother there is more to say—a story. She was from that same north Arkansas backwoods and had sisters and brothers. There was rumored to be Osage blood—oil-well Indians who'd lost it all. But I know almost nothing about my grandmother's parents, although I have a photograph of my great-grandmother and my grandmother together, along with my grandmother's new, second husband, all of them seated in a rustic farm wagon. My mother is in this picture, but in the back. It is a photo posed in a studio, possibly in Fort Smith in the mid-twenties. It is meant to be comic. My great-grandmother is old, grim, witchy-looking; my grandmother, stern and pretty in a long beaver coat; my mother young, with piercing dark eyes aimed straight at the camera. Nothing is particularly comic.

Essie, Bennie, Granny, and Edna, Fort Smith, Arkansas, 1928

AT SOME POINT SHE—MY GRANDMOTHER—had left her first husband, my mother's father, and taken up with the younger man in the picture, Bennie Shelley—a boxer and a roustabout. This may also have been in Fort Smith. He is a pretty, blond boy. Slim and quick and tricky. "Kid Richard" was his ring name. I am his namesake, though we are not otherwise related. My grandmother was older than Kid Richard. But to quickly marry him, she lied about her age, took a smooth eight years off, and almost immediately began to dislike having her pretty daughter—my mother—around.

And so for a period—everything in my mother's life seemed to happen for a period, never for long— she was sent off to live at the St. Anne's Academy. Again, in Fort Smith. This must've seemed like a good idea to her father, up in the mountains—but now no longer her guardian—because he paid her tuition to be taught by the nuns. I don't know what her mother—whose name was Essie or Lessie or just Les—did during the time my mother was in school. It was only three years—to grade nine. Possibly she tried to secure a firmer grip on Bennie Shelley, who was from Fayetteville and had family there. He'd worked as a waiter when he wasn't boxing, and soon went into the dining-car service on the Rock Island, which meant living in El Reno and as far out the line as Tucumcari. Unquestionably she sought to rule him and tried, with middling success, to do so all her life. She must've sensed she could go a long way with him and that he was her best and possibly last chance for something. A ticket out of the sticks.

My mother remarked often how much she'd liked the sisters at St. Anne's. They were severe. Knowledgeable. Imperious. Dedicated. But humorous, too. It was there, as a boarding student, that she gained what education she ever did. She was an average student but was liked, although she smoked cigarettes and was pretty and talked back, and was often punished. If she had never told me about the nuns, if their influence on her life hadn't been made clear to me, I might never have understood a great deal about my mother. St. Anne's cast both a light and a shadow into her later life. In her heart of hearts—as her Irish mother-in-law darkly suspected—my mother was a secret Catholic. Which meant (to her) that she was a forgiver. A respecter of rituals and protocols. Reverent about the trappings of faith and about inner disciplines, although she was uncertain about God. All I've ever thought about Catholics—good and not good—I first thought because of my mother, who was never one, but who lived among them at an impressionable age and liked what she learned and liked who taught her.

But for reasons I know nothing about, her mother—now demanding (shockingly) that her daughter be known as her *sister*—took her out of St. Anne's, mid-year. Which was it for school, even though my mother was not a welcome addition to *her* mother's life. I have never understood why her mother took her back. Money, conceivably. Just one of those unexplained acts that changes everything.

With her parents, now, there was moving. From north Arkansas to Kansas City. To El Reno again. To Davenport and Des Moines—wherever the Rock Island took Bennie, who was going forward in the dining-car service and turning himself into a go-getter. Soon, he would climb down off the railroad and take a job as a caterer at the Arlington Hotel in

Hot Springs, where he put my mother to work as cashier in the cigar stand, and where, for her, a view of a wider world opened a tiny inch. People from far away came to Hot Springs to take the bathing cures. Jews from Chicago and New York. Canadians speaking French. Europeans. Rich people—all of whom she sold cigars and newspapers to. Because she was pretty, she met baseball players. Big-league teams trained in the mountains there at that time. The Cardinals. The Cubs. She met Grover Alexander and Gabby Hartnett. And sometime during this period, when she was seventeen and living with her parents and working long hours, she also met my father, who clerked at the Clarence Saunders grocery on Central Avenue, and they fell in love.

About their courtship I know nothing except that it took place—in Hot Springs, but in Little Rock, too. This was 1927. My father was twenty-three. She was seventeen or eighteen. At the Saunders firm, he worked as a produce man—vegetables and fruit. Something had brought him down from the country where he was born, in Atkins—some restlessness. What he might've had in mind for himself, I don't know. But I can easily see them as a couple. Compatibly handsome. Friendly and shy. My mother, black-haired, dark-eyed, curvaceous. My father, blue-eyed like me, big, gullible, honest, conceding. And I can sense what they each might've thought about the other. My mother knew things—not all of them good. She'd worked in hotels, been wrested out of boarding school. Had lived in cities. Been around a wide mix of people, was an unwieldy third party to her mother's marriage. Whereas my father was a country boy who'd quit school in the seventh grade, was the baby of three, the sheltered son of a suicide. I can believe my mother wanted a better life than working for her slew-footed stepfather; that she believed she'd not been treated especially well and thought of her life, so far, as being somewhat rough; that she didn't like being her grudging mother's "sister" and was in danger of losing all expectation if something didn't happen. I can also easily believe my father simply saw my mother and wanted her—loved her immediately. What they each thought about the other was, *Here is someone good*.

They were married up in Morrilton by a justice of the peace, sometime early in 1928, and arrived at my father's mother's house in Atkins as newlyweds. There is no report of what anyone said. They had acted for themselves. Though from her new mother-in-law they both, without doubt, found disapproval.

IT WAS MY MOTHER'S SMALL BOAST that my father kept a job through the Depression, and that there was always money enough. They lived in Little Rock, and for a while my father advanced in his work as a grocer. He came to manage several Liberty stores and for a time pursued that as a future. Though around 1936 he was fired. No one ever told me why. They moved back to Hot Springs. And soon he took another job, this time selling laundry starch for the Faultless Company out of Kansas City. Huey Long had worked for them two decades earlier. It was traveling work, and the two of them made their married life together riding in his company car. New Orleans. Memphis. Texarkana. They lived in hotels, spent the few off-days back in Little Rock. My father called on wholesalers, prisons, hospitals, a leper colony in Louisiana. He sold starch by the box-car full. My mother never characterized that time then—the middle-to-late thirties—except to say that he and she'd had fun together—her word. Something about it all may have seemed un-narratable—unworthy or unnecessary for telling. Years on, her fleeting references to that time made the thirties seem like a long weekend. A loose, pick-up-and-go life. Drinking. Cars. Restaurants. Dancing. People they liked on the road. A life in the south. A swirling thing that didn't really have a place it was going. She sometimes gave the impression of possibly untidy things having gone on, some recklessness of spirit that didn't rise to the level of evil, yet something a son would be better off not to worry with. There must've been an abundance of lives like theirs. It seems "a period" to me now. A specific time, toward the beginning of the Second war. Though it was just their life.

They may also have begun to think they wouldn't

or couldn't have a child, because they *hadn't* had one. I don't know how much this mattered to them, if there were other pregnancies that didn't succeed, or if they were even "trying." It was not their way to fight fate, but to see life as much as possible as being okay. So that this time—being married without children—lasted on. Fifteen years. Although, looked at from the moment of my birth, 1944, all that life lived child-less, on the road, not paying much attention, may have come to seem to them—even if it was their only life—an odd time, possibly pointless in comparison to the pointedness of a life *with* a child.

ALL FIRST CHILDREN, certainly all only children, date the beginning of their lives as notable events. For my parents, my arrival came as a surprise, al-most simultaneous with the end of World War II—the event that finished the thirties in this country. And it came when, in essence, their young life was finishing. He was thirty-nine. She was thirty-three. You could say it was a moment when the intimacy they'd established was finally being brought forward to greater consequence—in this case to a life they may have all but abandoned any thought of because no children had come.

By all accounts, they were happy to have me. It may have been an event that made their life feel conventional for once, that settled them and made them think about matters their friends had thought about for years. Staying put. The future. They had never owned a house or had a car, except the car my father's job provided. They had never had to choose a "home," a place to be permanently. Only now they did, or could.

At the suggestion of my father's boss, they moved from the apartment in Little Rock they rarely stayed in, down and across the river to Mississippi, to Jackson, the center of my father's traveling territory, a place he could easily return to on weekends, since my mother wouldn't be going with him now. There was a baby, or soon would be.

They knew little of Mississippi, being Arkies. And they knew almost no one in Jackson—a couple of jobbers my father called on, and one salesman off the road. It could not have been an easy transition.

They rented an apartment in a brick duplex beside a school. They joined a church—the Presbyterians—found a grocery, the library, a bus stop. You could walk to the main street from 736 North Congress. There were neighbors—elderly, established, unbeckoning families hanging on in big, galleried homes in what was the older part of town. Still, quickly this became their life. Once I'd arrived, my mother stayed at home—alone with me—while my father went off to work Monday mornings and came back Friday nights. Our weekend visitor. It became a routine of days, afternoons, nights, sidewalks, dressing, feeding me, the radio, looking out the window—my mother a single, precise shadow in a snapshot of myself.

They had never exactly done anything like this—been apart, cared for a child. And between them, I don't know what happened. Given their characters, my best belief is that nothing dramatic did. That their life changed radically, that I was there now, that the future meant something different from what it *had* meant, that there was apparently no talk of other children, that they saw far less of each other—all that meant little to how they felt about each other, or to how they registered how they felt. Psychology was not a science they practiced any more than history was. They were not natural inquirers, did not often ask themselves how they felt about things. They simply found, if they had not known it before, that they'd signed on for the full tour. I don't think my mother longed for a more fulfilling career than this one or even a more active life. I don't think my father had other women on the road. I don't think the intrusion of me into their lives was anything they didn't think of as normal and at least as *all right*. Life was going this way now and not that way anymore. They loved each other. They loved me. Nothing else much mattered. They must've accommodated. One of my earliest memories is of my father moving around their sunny apartment on Monday mornings, packing his suitcase to leave, whistling "Zip-a-Dee-Doo-Dah, Zip-a-Dee-ay."

SO THEN, BECAUSE HE—MY FATHER—was now almost always away at work, the part of life that has

Richard and Edna, Jackson, Mississippi, 1945

largely to do with my mother. The end of the war and then Korea. Truman and Eisenhower, school, television, bicycles, one big snowstorm in 1949—the time when we were on North Congress, down from the Mississippi state capitol building, and next door to the Jefferson Davis School. The time when we lived in Jackson but also when *we went*. With him—as I've told it. Little Rock, New Orleans, etc. Christmas. Summers. The time of his first heart attack. Me being with them, but mostly being with her.

Chiefly, I remember pieces of life from then, at least to age sixteen—1960, the up-ending year for my mother and me, the year my father came awake in his bed on a Saturday morning and died, with me up onto his covers with him, breathing into his mouth, trying to help him, and my mother for a while losing the run of herself. There was a life's worth of small events. I have remembered more than I do now. I've written down memories, disguised salient events into novels, told stories again and again to keep them within my reach. But pieces can stand for the whole well enough. Though each must make a difference to me or I wouldn't remember them so well.

I remember an elderly neighbor stopping me once on the sidewalk and asking me matter-of-factly who I was. This was on Congress Street. Maybe I was nine or seven or five. It was a thing that could happen to you in Jackson. But when I said my name—Richard Ford—she said, "Oh, yes. Your mother's the cute little black-haired woman up the street." These were words that immediately affected me, and strongly, since they proposed my first conception of my mother as someone else, as someone whom other people saw and considered and not *just* as my mother. A cute woman, which she wasn't. Black-haired, which she was. She *was* five feet five inches tall, but I never have known if that is tall or short. I think I must have believed, as I still do, that it was normal. I remember this, however, as a sentinel moment in life. Small but important. It alerted me to my mother's—what?—public side. To the aspect of her that other people saw and dealt with and that was always there, alongside what I saw. I don't believe I ever thought of her again without thinking of that, or ever addressed her except with that knowledge. That she was Edna

Edna and Parker, Jackson, Mississippi, 1953

Ford, a person who was my mother but who was also someone else.

It is, of course, a good lesson to learn early—cute, little, black-haired, five-five—since one of the premier challenges for us all is to know our parents fully—assuming they survive long enough, are worth knowing, and it is physically possible. The more we see our parents fully, after all, see them as the world does, the better our chances to see the world as *it* is.

There was the flat tire we all three had, halfway across the Mississippi bridge at Greenville. High up there, over the river. I have mentioned it earlier. My mother stayed in the car with me while my father got out to fix things, and she held me so tightly to her I could barely breathe. I was four or three. Later she always said, "I smothered you when you were little. You were all we had. I'm sorry." And then she'd tell me the bridge story again. But I wasn't sorry—have never been. We were way up there, after all. It was terrifying. *Smothering* meant to me, *Here is danger. Love protects you.* These are words I respect. I'm not comfortable on high bridges now, but I have come to my fear from the recesses of my mother's love.

I also remember my mother having a hysterectomy and my grandfather—her stepfather—Bennie Shelley, joking cruelly about it *to her*—about what good "barbers" the nuns at St. Dominic's Hospital had been. Barbers. Nuns—whom she so admired. For years to come, I didn't understand what he'd meant. He reflected this lewd aspect all his days. It made her cry.

I REMEMBER ONCE, in our front yard on Congress, something unsettling happened, something I said or did. I don't know what. I might've been six and already had an urge to say disruptive things. But, in response to whatever I said, my mother just suddenly began running away from me—out across our yard and onto the school grounds next door. Just running away, her flowery cotton dress flapping in the warm breeze. Naturally it frightened me, and I shouted out, "No, no, no, no!" But she disappeared past the back corner of the school building and was gone. I've never known how serious she was about needing to escape. Eventually she came back. But I have always understood from this event that there might be reasons to run away. In her case—alone, with a small child, in a strange city, knowing no one. That could be enough.

There were two fights they had that I was present for. One on St. Louis Street, in the French Quarter in New Orleans. I have mentioned this. It was in front of Antoine's Restaurant. I think they were both drunk, though I didn't know what drunk was. One of them wanted to go to a bar and have a drink after dinner. The other didn't and insisted on going back to the hotel. This was in 1955. We had tickets to the Sugar Bowl—Navy versus Ole Miss. They yelled at each other, and my father yanked my mother's arm and pressed her against a brick wall, after which they walked back separately. Later we all got in bed together in the Monteleone and no one stayed mad. In our family no one nagged or held grudges or nursed anger, though we could all *get* angry and often did.

The other fight was somewhat worse. It was near

the same time as the other—possibly a difficult period for them. Again, they were drinking. My father had invited friends over to our house in Jackson, but my mother hadn't been consulted and didn't like it. All the lights were on, as usual. They were both combustible by nature. Again, she swore and raised her voice and pointed accusingly at the front door. I remember the guests standing outside the screen, gaping in—confused. I remember their white faces and my mother shouting at them to get the hell out, though they were not even in. Presently these people left, and my father again held my mother's shoulders up against a wall by our bathroom and yelled at her while she struggled to get free. I remember the volume of what they angrily said, but not the words. I remember how hot it was—the porch light dimly on. No one got hit. No one ever did, except me when I was spanked or whipped. They just yelled and struggled for a while. Fought that way. Then later, when we were all in bed, with me in the middle between them, my father began to cry. "Boo-hoo-hoo. Boo-hoo-hoo." Those were the sounds he made, as if he'd learned how to cry from reading it in a book.

And there was one more thing. My mother, who had taught young girls to be young wives, did not excel at those skills herself. She disliked cleaning and ironing and cooking—from all their years on the road—and didn't do any of it well or any more than she had to. Consequently, often on hot summer days we would leave the house at noon, and walk up the block and across North State, and down to the Jitney Jungle grocery. (I never knew why it was called that.) There, it was air-conditioned, and you could get in line and buy a hot lunch from the steam-table, standing, the two of us, beside the neighbors we didn't know, all of us holding paper tickets with a number, waiting our turn to order—baked egg-plant, creamed corn, lima beans, collards, a pork chop, with banana pudding for dessert—the usual southern repast. One day as we were waiting among the others, my mother said to me, "Richard, do you see that woman standing over there?" I looked and saw a woman, someone I didn't know—tall and smiling, chatting with people, laughing. My mother looked at the woman again with a private expression I think now was estimating. I said yes. And my mother said, "That's Eurdora Welty. She's a writer." Which was information that meant nothing to me, except that it meant something to my mother, who sometimes read bestsellers in bed at night. I don't know if she had ever read something Eudora Welty wrote. I don't know if the woman *was* Eudora Welty, or was someone else. My mother may have wanted it to be Eudora Welty for reasons of her own. Possibly this event could seem significant now, in view of my life to come. But it didn't, then. I was only eight or nine. To me, it was just another piece in a life of pieces.

WHEN MY FATHER DIED, of course, everything changed—many things, it's odd to say, for the better where I was concerned. But not for the better where my mother was concerned. Nothing for her would be quite good again after February 20th, 1960. They'd had me and loved me. But to her my father had been everything. So that when he suddenly died, all that had been naturally implicit in her life either vanished or became different and explicit and not very good.

And she, who was not truly skilled at life without him—having never had a good life without him—became not very interested in life itself. And in a way that I see now and saw almost as clearly then, she gave up on the part of herself that loved him.

Not long after my father's funeral, when I was back in school and the neighbors had stopped calling and visiting and bringing over dishes of food—when grief and mourning had become indistinguishable—my mother sat me down and became specific about the formal features of her life now. She was fifty, she said. Her husband was dead. She had a son (me) who seemed mostly all right, but was veering into law scrapes, and so she needed to pay attention. We were now going to have to be more independent. Of him, certainly, because he was gone. But of each other, too. She was going to have to get a job. I was only sixteen, but she would not be able to look after me as she had. We agreed that I had a future, and that we would try to look after each other. But I would have to look after me now. We would be partners is what I remember thinking. My father, as I've told, had never been around much because of his work, and this new absence—death—was, for me, not so strongly felt as even I imagined it would be. I already, in fact, felt more in charge of myself. So a partnership with my mother, one in which she would not notice me so closely, seemed like a good arrangement. I was to stay out of jail because she didn't want to have to get me out. *Couldn't get me out,* she said. I was to find friends I could rely on. I could have a car of my own. I could go away in the summers to find a job in Little Rock with my grandparents and return to school in Jackson in the fall. I was freer but would have to be more responsible. She was trying not to state too much. She didn't want *everything* to have to be explicit, since so much was. Whereas when my father was alive so little had needed to be. Not being too explicit would give her a chance and time to adjust. To think about things. To become whatever she could—or would *have* to become—in order to get along from there on out.

I don't remember the exact chronological order of things, commencing now. 1960, '61, '62. Time whirled by. I was a tenth grader and on. But I did not get brought before the juvenile court again. I did live summers with my grandparents, who ran their big hotel in Little Rock. My grandfather bought me a black '57 Ford, which fairly quickly got stolen. I got beaten up a time or two, and then got some new friends. I did what I was told, in other words. I started to grow up in a hurry.

I think of that time—the time between my father's death and the time I left for Michigan to go to college—as a time when I didn't see my mother nearly as much as I once had. Though that is not exactly how it was. She was there. I was there. But I cannot discount my own adjustments to my father's death and absence, and to my new independence. I may have been more dazed than grieved, and it is true the new friends I found took me up. My mother got a job doing something at a company that made school pictures. This required training. And it was then—again, when she was fifty—that she may have felt the first full effects of having been made to leave school in 1925. Though she finished the training, got along and did not have trouble and began coming home tired every day. But then she left that job and became a rental agent for a new, high-rise apartment house in Jackson. Sterling Towers. Later, she tried to get the job as manager but didn't get it. Who knows why? She then took another job as night cashier in a hotel, the Robert E. Lee. This job she kept maybe a year. And after that she was hired to be an admitting clerk in the emergency room at the University of Mississippi Hospital, a job she liked very much and was good at because she was sympathetic and businesslike, and the doctors liked her.

And there was at least one boyfriend during that time. A married man, from Tupelo, named Matt Matthews, who lived in the apartment building where she had worked as the rental agent. He was a big, bluff, good-natured man, possibly in the furniture business, who drove a Lincoln Continental with an automatic pistol strapped to the steering column. I liked him. I liked it that my mother liked him. It didn't matter that he was married—not to me and, I guess, not to my mother. I really have no idea about what was between them, what they did alone. He took her on drives. Flew her to Memphis in his airplane. Acted respectfully toward both of us.

She may have told me she was just passing time with him, getting her mind off her woes, letting someone be nice to her. We both knew that nothing she told me about him had to match the truth. I sometimes wished that she could marry him. And at other times I was content to have them be lovers, if that's what they were. He had sons near my age. Later I would meet them and like them. But this was long after he and my mother were finished.

What finished them was brought on by me but was not completely my doing. Matt had faded for a time. His business brought him into Jackson less, and he was often away for months. My mother had quit talking about him, and our life had returned to its almost-normal level, the level of having my father be dead. I was having my usual bitter time in school— getting an F in algebra (I'd already failed once) and having no ideas about how I could improve. My mother was cashiering nights at the Robert E. Lee and coming home by eleven.

But then one night she didn't come home. I had a test the next day. Algebra. And I must've been in an agitated state of mind. I called the hotel and

heard that she had left on time. And for some reason this scared me. I got in my Ford and drove down
to the street by the hotel—Griffith Street—a fringe
neighborhood near a black section of town, where I
thought she might not be safe. I drove around until
I found her car, the gray-and-pink Oldsmobile '88
that had been my father's last car and his pride and
joy. It was parked under some crepe myrtle, across
from Sterling Towers, where Matt kept his place—
something I knew about, since it was how they'd
met. It was close to the hotel. And for some reason I
must've panicked. There was no clear reason to, but
I did. I'm not sure what I thought, but thinking of it
now I believe I only wanted to ask Matt—if he was
there—if he knew where my mother was. This may
be right, though it's possible, too, that I knew she
was there and wanted to make her leave.

I went into the building. It must've been near
midnight. There was no security guard. I found
Matt's name on the directory and went up the elevator and down the hall to his door. And I banged on it.
I hit the door very hard with my fists. Then I waited.

Matt opened the door, and my mother was

there in the room behind him. She had a drink in her hand. Lights were on low, and she was standing in the middle of the room. Nothing was out of order. It was a nice apartment. Both of them were shocked—by me. And I was already ashamed to be there. But I was, I think, terrified. Not that she was there. Or that I was alone. But just that I didn't know what in the hell. Where was she? What else was I going to have to lose?

I remember being out of breath. I was seventeen years old. I can't remember much of what anybody said or did except me, briefly. "Where have you been?" I said to her, behind him—or I said words to that effect. "I didn't know where you were. That's all."

And that *was* all. All of that. Matt said very little. My mother immediately got her coat. "Oh, Richard, for God's sake," she said. "Go home." We both went home, in two cars. In the house, she acted annoyed at me, and I *was* mad at her. We talked. Eventually she told me she was sorry, and I told her I didn't care if she saw Matt, only that she should tell me when she'd be home late. She said she would. To my knowledge she never saw Matt Matthews or any other man again as a lover for as long as she lived.

Later, years later, when she was dying, I tried to explain it all to her again—my part, what I thought, *had* thought—as if we could still open it and repair that night. All she needed to do was call me or, even now—years later—say she *would've* called me. But that was not how she saw it. She just looked impatient and shook her head, in her hospital bed. "Oh *that*," she said. "My God. That was just silliness. You had no business coming up there. You were out of your mind. I just saw, though, that I couldn't be doing things like that. I had a son to raise." She looked disgusted, at everything—all the cards the fates had dealt her—a no-good childhood, my father, then his death, me, her own inability to vault over all of it to a better life. It was another proof of something bad, the likes of which I believe she felt she'd had plenty.

Eventually she sold the suburban house my father had bought and greatly prized, and moved us into a different high-rise. Magnolia Towers. I was provided a tutor for math, and did better. She was switching jobs again. I registered these changes, but not vividly. Though based on what I know now about such things, not much was easy for her. Even though there might've been a part of it all that she—not exactly enjoyed but—took satisfactions from. Small accomplishments. We did not fight, as we had when I was younger. Instead, we adjusted to one another almost as adults would. We grew wry and humorous with each other. We cast glances, gave each other looks. We were rarely ironic or indirect or crafty with anger. We didn't know these would be among the last times we would ever live together. We just somehow knew how we were supposed to act as widowed mother and only teenage son, and took self-conscious pleasure in acting that way. In retrospect, I think it was a way of living not so different from when my father was alive. Only of course he wasn't.

I did not, and do not now, know about our money. My father had had a little insurance, but there was no pension from his job. Faultless Starch was not that kind of company. Maybe some money was saved in a bank. My grandparents came forward to help. They

Edna and Richard, New Orleans, 1974

had made money and had lent my father money for the new house. I know the government paid money for me as a dependent child, until I was eighteen. But I mean only to say I didn't and don't precisely know how much my mother needed to be working; how much money was required to come through; if we had debts, creditors. It may have been we didn't, and that she went to work just to thrust herself in the direction life seemed to be taking—toward independence. Solitariness. All that *that* meant.

There were memorable moments. When my Ford was stolen, my mother and I went one winter day after school, just at dusk, out to a dealership across the Pearl River in Rankin County, where bargains were supposedly waiting. She felt we should replace my car, and so did I. But when we were there looking at cheap models for me, she saw a new black Thunderbird and stood staring at it. I knew that was what she really wanted—for herself—that it would make her feel better to own it. Getting my father's Olds out of our lives would help with our adjustments. There was no one there then to tell us not to. It was part of our new, unasked-for freedom.

I told her she should buy the Thunderbird. I could do without a car in high school. She stared at it for a long time, eventually got in and tilted the steering wheel, shut the door a few times, pushed the pedals. Then we left with the promise to the salesman that she would think about it. Though in a few days, when the police had found my old car, she decided just to keep the Olds a while longer.

Another time was when my girlfriend and I had been experimenting inexpertly with one kind of sexual pleasure and another—inside my car. We knew almost nothing about sex. But just out of the blue, my girlfriend—who was from Texas—decided that she was now definitely pregnant (though we hadn't yet driven away from where we were parked) and that her life was now ruined. Mine, I knew the instant she said this, certainly *felt* ruined. There was evidence aplenty of kids in our school marrying at fourteen, having babies, being divorced. This was the south.

I once again found myself in terror. And when I got home—it was the very same Sunday afternoon—I abandoned myself to my mother; told her *all* we'd been doing just one hour before, all we hadn't. I

spoke in details, methodically, horribly of anatomi-
cal parts and positions, extents and degrees. What I
wanted from her was to know if my girlfriend *could*
be pregnant, based on what she knew about these
things. (How much could that really have been?)
These were all matters a boy should take up with
his father. Though I wouldn't have. Such a conver-
sation would've dumbfounded my poor father, then
silenced him. In any case he was gone.

My mother was the only one there. I knew her
very well—at least I acted that way and she did, too.
She was fifty-two. I was eighteen. She was practiced
with me, knew the kind of boy I was. We were, as
stated, partners in my messes and hers. I sat on the
couch in our apartment and painfully, painstakingly
told her what scared me, told her what I couldn't get
worked out in my thinking, went through it all more
than once; used the words *it, hers, inside.* She, stifling
her dread, calmly assured me that everything was
going to be fine. Nobody got pregnant doing what
we were doing. It was all a young girl's scare fanta-
sies. Not to worry. So I didn't.

Of course, she was wrong. She couldn't possibly have been wronger. My girlfriend did *not* get pregnant, but only because an indifferent fate intervened. Thousands of girls get pregnant doing what we were doing. Thousands get pregnant doing less. My mother either didn't know much, or else knew a great, great deal: knew that what was done was done, and that all the worry and explaining and getting-things-straight wouldn't matter now. If I escaped ruin and shame, it was good luck. I should be more careful in the future if I was to have my future. And that was about it. If my girlfriend *had been* pregnant, what anybody thought, believed or said wouldn't matter very much. Life would go the way it went.

And there is of course, a lesson in that, too—one I have tried over time and not usually successfully to have guide me: the lesson that says, it's what *happens* that matters, more than what people, even yourself, think about what happens before or after. It mostly only matters what we *do*. I had not then, and have not yet, looked at the world through eyes like hers. Possibly fuller understanding will come. It was my mother, though, who taught this to me first.

In 1962, I went away to college at Michigan State. My mother neither encouraged nor discouraged this. It was a choice of mine and no one else's. Going to a college in Mississippi didn't enter my mind. I wanted distance by then, and to be a hotel manager like my grandfather, Ben Shelley, who had done well at it. Michigan State was the place to learn about hotels. I do not remember my mother and me talking about college—though we must've. She hadn't been to one and didn't know much about what went on there. She was interested, but in a way that didn't seem vital or supervisory. Maybe she thought I wouldn't like it and would come home soon. Maybe she thought I would never go, even when Michigan State accepted me and I said I was going. Maybe she thought Michigan wasn't so far from Mississippi, which is both true and not true. Or maybe she thought nothing, or nothing that was clear; just noticed that I was doing this and that, sending off and receiving letters, establishing dates, and decided she would cross the bridge to college when the time came. The assumption became that I was going. Money would be found somewhere.

In late September, then, she and I together got on the Illinois Central at the Union Station in Jackson and rode to Chicago (our first such long trip as mother and son, though we had ridden shorter distances in years past to meet my father in places where he was working). In Chicago, we transferred crosstown from the old Central Station to Dearborn Street and the Grand Trunk, and rode over to Lansing. She wanted to go with me. I think she wanted to see all that. Michigan. Illinois. Cornfields. White barns. The Middle West. Wanted to see from a train window what went on there, how that was, what it all looked like up north, possibly detect why I seemed to want it and how I would situate myself among those people, live in their buildings, eat their food, learn their lingo. Find out why this was where I had chosen to go. Her son. This was how she saw her duty and our partnership unfolding.

And, too, some indulgence in the ordinary may have been what she wanted: to accompany her son to college, to fashion a send-off; to see herself and me, for a moment, fitted into a pattern of what others were up to, what people in general did. If that could happen to her, to us, then maybe some normal life could reconvene, since she could not have thought of her life as very normal at that time—two years away from my father's death.

We spent a week together in East Lansing. Late September 1962. She had never been so far from home. And when I had enrolled, been assigned my classes, invaded my dormitory room, met my roomies, and she and I had spent a couple of leisurely days touring and roaming, eating restaurant dinners across from one another until nothing was left to say—when that was over, she and I went back to the GTW station, and I stood up on a bus-stop bench beside the train tracks, and held up my arms in the cool, snapping air so she would see me as the train pulled away toward Chicago. I saw her, her white face behind the tinted window, her palm flat to the glass for me to see. And she was crying. *Good-bye*, she was saying. I waved my hand, a wide wave, and mouthed, *Good-bye. I love you*, and watched her train go out of sight through the warp of that bricky old factory town. At that moment I suppose you could say I started my life alone-in-earnest, and that whatever was left of my childhood ended.

FOLLOWING WHICH, the life that would take us forward together as adults began. An even more fragmented, truncated life of visits long and short. Letters. Phone calls. Telegrams. Meetings in cities far from home. Conversations in cars, in airports, train stations. Efforts to see each other. Leaving dominating everything—my growing older and her growing older, both observed from varying distances.

She held out alone in Mississippi for another year, moved back into the duplex on Congress Street, rented out the other side. She worked on at the hospital, where for a time, I think, the whole new life she'd been handed came together. I am speculating because I was gone to college and would stay gone. She said she liked her job, liked the young interns at the hospital, liked the drama of the ER, liked working. In my view, from my distance, she experienced capability for the first time, separate from her skills as a wife and my mother. It may have started to be satisfactory that I was away. It may have seemed that there *was* a life to lead, and that under the circumstances she had done reasonably well with her fate. She might ease up, let events happen without fearing the worst. One bad thing *could* finally turn into something less bad.

This, at least, is what I wanted to think. How an only son feels about his widowed mother whom he loves but is far away from, is necessarily an involved business. But it is not oversimplifying to say that he wants good to come to her. In all these years, the years of curtailed life with my mother, I was aware that things would never be completely *all right* with her. Partly it was a matter of her choosing; partly it was a matter of her character—of just how she could see *any* life without my father, with so much life left to be lived in an un-ideal way. Always somewhere down deep she seemed resigned. I could never plumb her without coming to that stop point—a point where widening expectation simply ceased. This is not to say she was always unhappy. Or that she never laughed. (I could make her laugh; others could.) Or that she didn't see life as life, didn't regain parts of herself. She did. Only, not utterly. Not in the way a mother could disguise from her son. I always saw it. Always felt it. Always experienced her unease with life. Her resisting it.

From almost the first moment in the room where he had died, I felt my father's death surrendering back to me nearly as much as it took away. His sudden departure, the great, unjust loss of his life, handed me a life to live by my own designs, freed me to my own decisions. A boy could do worse than to lose his father—even a good father—just when the world begins to array itself all around him. And because I thought this way, I wished my mother could relent more than she could. But it was not that way for her, even if I can't exactly imagine how it *was*. She had talents. She was intuitive, passionate, candid, quick-witted, mirthful, occasionally fiery and dire. And decent. And yet I can say that in all her time in life after my father died, the twenty-one years that she would be without him, her life never seemed fully lived. She took trips—to Mexico, to New York, to California, to Banff, to various warm islands. She had friends who doted on her and whom she spoke highly of and enjoyed. She had an increasingly easy life as her own parents died. Eventually she had us—my wife and me—who loved her and included her in everything possible. But when I would say to her—and I did say—"Mother, are you enjoying your life? Are things all right?" she would look at me with familiar impatience and roll her eyes. "Richard, I'm never going to be ecstatic. It's not in my nature. Concentrate on *your* life. Leave mine alone. I'll take care of me."

And that, I think, is what she did after his death and my departure, when she was on her own. She maintained, made an objective out of that. She became brisk, businesslike, more self-insistent. Her already deep voice became deeper, assumed a kind of acquired gravity that matched her outlook. She drank in the evenings to get a little drunk, and took up an everyday attitude of one kind of firmness or another—particularly toward men, whom she began to view as liabilities. She made her situation be the custom and cornerstone of her public self.

She would not be taken advantage of, even though I suspect no one wanted to take advantage of her. A widow had to look out though, had to pay attention to all details. No one could or would help you. A life lived efficiently wouldn't save you, but it would prepare you for what you couldn't be saved from.

Along the way she helped maintain my wife and me when we were young and newly married—always at a prudent distance and only as we needed it. She eventually sold the house on Congress, moved back to Little Rock and into my grandparents' hotel, and lived comfortably with them until Bennie suddenly died, after which she lived with her mother in apartments here and there in town, as her mother gradually grew ill, then crippled, then house-bound, but never appreciative. She became a daughter again at fifty-five, one who looked after an irascible mother who'd once wanted her to be her "sister." She did not relish it.

They had, the two of them, plenty of money. A good car. There was a set of friends—mostly widowed—people in their stratum. Her mother "accompanied" her everywhere. They went to eat in small groups, played canasta afternoons, spoke to people on the phone, watched soap operas, engaged in arguments, grew bored, restive, furious. Had cocktails. Laughed about men. Stared. Lived a nice and comfortable life of waiting.

Our life together during this time—mother and son—consisted mainly of my knowledge of what her life was and her knowledge of mine. And visits. After college, we continued to live far away from each other. She in Little Rock. I, and then I and Kristina, in Michigan, California, Mexico, Chicago, Michigan again, New York, New Jersey, Vermont. To visit us she arrived on trains and planes and in cars, ready to take us to dinner but also to loan us money. To have a room painted. Buy tires for our car. Pay a doctor bill. To worry about me. To listen. To be present for a little while as a part of what passed for our family—wherever we were—and then to go home.

It must be true for most of us to believe that our particular circumstances are not exactly typical of what the mass of others' lives are like. Not better. Not worse. Only peculiar in *some* way. My mother's and my life *did* seem peculiar. Or possibly it just seemed imperfect. Being so far from each other. Her being alone. Our visits and partings. All without either of us knowing what *perfect* could've been—my father not being dead of course. But more than that, too.

This imperfect arc of events consumed, as I've said, twenty years of both our lives—her last twenty, my second—when whatever my life was to be was beginning and then happening. It never felt exactly right that during all these years I could not see my mother more, that we did not have a day-to-day life. That I lived at a great distance by choice. That the repairs we made to things after my father's death could not be finished and shared. And that at no time was there a moment when life for us rejoined itself and became as it had been before he died. This imperfection underlay everything. So that when she left me again and again and again, she would cry. And that is what she cried about. That what we had together was most of all there was. And it was not enough. Not a full enough *outcome*. She told me that once in the elevator where she lived, a new acquaintance had asked her, "Mrs. Ford, do you have any children?"

And without thinking she had said, "No." And then she'd thought to herself, *Oh, for God's sake. Of course I do. There's Richard.*

Our conversations over these years came to have much to do with television, with movies we'd seen and hadn't, with books she was reading, with baseball—which she adored. The subject of Johnny Bench and Jackie Robinson—whom she admired—came up often. After my grandmother died, my wife and I took my mother to the World Series at Yankee Stadium, where she rooted for the Dodgers, whom we didn't like, and complained about the seats we'd moved mountains to get. We took her on the Universal Studios Tour. We took her back to Antoine's in New Orleans, where we did not discuss the fight she'd had with my father in 1955. We drove her to California and to Montreal and Yellowstone. To Maine. To Vermont. To northern Michigan. To wherever we went and *could* take her. We, she and I, observed each other. She observed Kristina and our marriage and liked them both. She observed my efforts to be a writer and supported them, but did not understand why I was doing it. "When are you going to get a job and get started?" she asked me once, after I'd published two novels and was teaching at Princeton. She observed the fact that Kristina and I had no children but offered no opinion—though I'm certain she had several. She silently estimated her life, and her life with ours, and possibly did not completely see how one gave rise to the other but accepted that it did.

I noticed of course that she grew older; knew that her life was not very much to her liking but that she made the most of its surfaces. She would sometimes take me aside early on a morning when we could be alone together, two adults, and say to me: "Richard, are you happy?" And when I told her I was, she would say in a warning voice, "You *must* be happy. That's so important." Not that she was unhappy, but just that she knew whereof she spoke.

And that is the way life went on. Not pointlessly. But not pointedly, either. Maybe this is also usual in our lives with our older parents—a feeling that some goal is being sought, and then the recognition of what that goal inevitably is, after which we return our attention to what's present now.

Something, however, some essence of my and my mother's life is not, I realize, coming clear through these words—as if there are not words and memory enough to give a life back and have it be right. In one sense, over our years lived apart, my mother and I acted toward one another the way people do who *like* each other very much and want to see each other more. Special friends. But then I have not said about her that she never interfered, that she agreed that my life with Kristina had retired a large part of her motherhood. I have also not said that she didn't cultivate random, impromptu judgments about my life. That she always saw her visits as welcome—which they were. She saw, in fact, that what we'd made of things together— herself and me—was the natural result of events that were *themselves* natural. As before, she was not a psychologist. Not a student of life. Not a quizzer. But by some strange understanding—and maybe these are the words—she knew that we both knew that this was life. This is what we would have. We were not fatalists as mother and son. We made the best of things and knew we were doing that.

Richard and Kristina, Coahoma, Mississippi, 1984

IN 1973, MY MOTHER DISCOVERED she had breast cancer. It's tempting to say that such an ominous occurrence would inevitably follow a certain course for her and for people *like* her, people of her background and age—sixty-three: first there would be a time of being aware that something irregular was *there* inside her breast—something she didn't care to discuss with anyone or seek medical advice about. Then would follow a time of worry and growing realization and expectancy, during which a whole year would manage to pass. Followed by a casual mention to a trusted friend (who in this case unforgivably did nothing). Finally a distraught admission, to Kristina, with instructions not to tell anyone—me. Though of course she does tell me, after which we bring my mother quickly to a doctor who advises tests but because a year has passed does not seem hopeful.

What I remember of that brief, fraught period, which took place in Little Rock, is that following the first doctor visit, but before all the results were known, the contingencies stated and plans made, she and I and Kristina took the weekend together. (There is always somehow a weekend to wait.) She would "go in" on Monday for a definitive "proce-dure." Still, on Saturday it seemed a good idea to drive up to the country, to Atkins, to visit my fa-ther's sister and his cousins, whom she liked. To visit his grave. She told the sister—Viva—that she would be having these tests. And my aunt—who was much older than my mother—put a good face on it. Hugged her. Afterward, in my mother's Buick, we drove around the flat, Arkansas River bottom-land, which my father's father had lost be-fore he killed himself, but where none of the three of us had ever felt at home. But it didn't matter where we were. We knew this was the last of yet another period, a period when we could be the selves we had made up and tried to enact in the face of all that had gone before. Something in the tests would change everything—again—and we wanted to act out our conviction that, yes, this has been a life, this adroit coming and going, this health, this humor, this af-fection expressed in fits and starts, even this oc-casional sadness. Nothing would change that. We could look back, and it would seem like we were alive enough through it all.

DEATH STARTS A LONG TIME ahead of when it arrives. Even in death's very self there is life that has to be lived out.

My mother had cancer, but we found that the life we had confirmed that weekend could carry us further on. There were seven years to go, but we didn't know that. So we went quickly back to how we had done things. Visiting. Talking on the phone. Trips, friends, occasions. There was a more pressing need now to know from her "how things are," and the staunch willingness to have them be all right. To insisting, in other words, on life's being life, and recognizing that it could easily be less but shouldn't be. To us it *seemed* like the time that had gone before. Just not exactly.

My mother, I think, made the best of her problems. She had one breast removed. She took radiation but not chemotherapy. She went back to her solitary life in Little Rock. All accomplished with a minimum of exhibited fear and a great deal of stoicism, even humor—lessons first learned from the nuns, long ago. She bought a prosthesis, which she joked about. It seemed as if her years since my father's death had been training for bad news—for facing down disaster. She was, I think, sharply aware of how she was coping.

This was the first time I thought seriously that my mother might eventually come to live with us, which had been a well-discussed subject between her and me, there having been precedent for it and plenty of opportunity for us each to have a point of view. My mother's attitude was clear. She was against it. Such decisions ruined lives, spoiled the future, she thought. She had lived with her own begrudging mother, and that had eventuated in years of arid unhappiness. Bickering. Impasse. Her mother had disliked her for it, she said, had hated being looked after. She'd turned even meaner. It was a no-win, and she wanted no part of it, wanted me to swear off the idea. Which I did. We laughed about how high and dry I would someday leave her. How she would be in the poorhouse, and I'd be living it up someplace far away. France. Farting through silk, was the old Arkie saying.

She was, herself, practical. She made arrangements in someplace called Presbyterian Village, in

Little Rock. *There* would be her home when she was ready. She wrote out a big check to them against the day, reserved a place for whenever. They promised to do their duty. My wife and I saw this as an acceptable, even a good arrangement. "I don't want to have to be at anybody's mercy," my mother said. And that was that.

So it was back *again* to regular life, as regular as could be. Life in remission. Kristina and I had moved to New Jersey. We owned a nice house. And there were plenty more visits, with my mother doing most of the visiting—spending afternoons out in our shady yard, chatting up our Orthodox neighbors as if she knew all about them, weeding our flower beds. Raking leaves. Sitting in the gazebo. She seemed whole. In high spirits. Illness and the possibility of illness had made her seize life harder. She wanted to do more. Visit Hawaii. Go on cruises. She began to go to church more regularly. Became a deacon. She had new friends, younger than she was. We heard about them by name. Blanche. Herschel. Mignon. Louise. People we never met, but who drank and laughed and liked her and were liked by her. I had pictures of them in my mind. Loud, personable southerners.

The year was now measured from medical exam to medical exam, always in the late winter, soon after my birthday. Every year there was good news delivered, after worrying. And every year there was a time to celebrate and feel a reprieve.

I do not mean to say that our lives—the three of us—were lived outside the expectation and prism of death. For her, definitely not. The joy of surviving was tainted by the squeamish certainty that you can't survive. And no one can lose one parent and not live out his life waiting for the other to drop dead or begin to die. I read my mother's death in almost all her life's evidence during those days and short years. I looked for illness. Listened to her complaints too carefully. Planned her death obscurely in my abhorrence of it—treated myself to it early so that when the time came I would not go down completely.

At first there were backaches. It is hard to remember exactly when. The winter of 1981, possibly—six years since her surgery. She came up to New Jersey to visit, and something had gone wrong. She was seventy-one, but pain had now come into her life. She looked worn down, invaded by hurting—though shortly before she'd been fine. She'd seen her doctors in Little Rock, but none of this had to do with her cancer, she said they said. It was back trouble. Her parts were just wearing out. She flew home from Princeton, but in the summer she hurt more. I would call her, and the phone would ring a long time, and then her answering voice would be weak, sometimes barely audible. "I hurt, Richard," she'd tell me, wherever I was. "The doctor is giving me these pills. But they don't always work." "I'll come down there," I always said. "No. I'll be fine," she'd say. "Do what you have to do." The summer managed past that way, and the fall began.

I started a teaching job in Massachusetts. And then one morning there was a call. It was just at light. I didn't know why anyone would call anyone at that hour—unless a death was involved, but that didn't seem possible. My mother had come into the hospital the night before, a nurse said from Little Rock—in an ambulance. She had been in serious pain. And when she got there her heart had paused, though it had started again. She was better now, the nurse assured me. I said I'd come that day, from Massachusetts; find people to teach my classes, drive to the airport in Albany. Which was what I did.

In Little Rock it was summer. Hot September. A friend of my mother's, a man named Ed Lingo—Louise's husband, it turned out—met me and drove me in. We went by old buildings, over railroad tracks, and across the Arkansas River past where my grandparents' hotel had been, but now was gone—imploded. Ed Lingo was in a mood to counsel me. Though this would not turn out well, he said. My mother had been sicker than I knew, had spent days and days in her apartment without coming out. She had been in bed all summer, he said. It was something I needed to prepare myself for. Her death.

But it was more than her death, he was predicting. Life—hers in particular, ours—was moving into a new class of event now. These things could be understood, is what he meant to say but didn't exactly. To hold out against them was hopeless and maybe perverse. This all was coming to be *a kind of thing that happens.* An inevitability. Best to see it that way.

Which, I suppose, is what I began to do. Our ride in the car, across town to the hospital, was a de-marking line. A man I hardly knew was suggesting to me how I should look at many important things; how I should consider my own mother, my own life, my future. Suggesting that I begin to see my *self* differently. That I stand back. It would be better.

You can mistake such moments as these, but at your own risk.

My mother, it turned out, *was* feeling better. But something unusual had happened. Her heart had, in fact, entirely stopped. There was congestion in her lungs, the doctor told me and told her in my presence. He was a small, curly-headed, bright-eyed young man in a white coat. Dr. Wilson. He was soft-spoken. He liked my mother. Everyone liked my mother. He remembered how she'd looked when she first came to see him. Years ago now. "Healthy."

In her hospital room, however, where we all three were, he sat down in a chair with some papers and told us even more bad news. Though it was just the customary bad news. He had performed other tests, and their results weren't good. He felt confused now, he said, by the course of a disease he supposedly knew all about. But the back pain was cancer. She was going to die, although he didn't know when she would. Sometime in the next year, he imagined. There didn't seem to be any thought of recovering. I know he was sorry to know it and have to say it. His job may even have been harder than ours was—though only on that day.

I do not really remember what we said to him. I'm sure we asked very good questions, since we were both good when the chips were down. I do not remember my mother crying or even seeming shocked. I did not cry. We knew, both of us, what class of event *this* was—this message. Among other things, this was the class of event that ended one long kind of uncertainty. I cannot believe we both, in our own ways, didn't feel some relief—as if one tired, old curiosity had been satisfied and other new curiosities were being ushered in. The obvious question—how serious is all this?—can be dispensed with in a hurry: the very worst. But it is an odd and un-obvious sensation to have—this relief. I wonder if doctors know how instinctive it is.

And still, in a way, even this news did not change things. The persuasive power of normal life is extravagant. To accept less than life when less is not overwhelmingly upon you is—at least for some— unacceptable.

My mother and I had several talks. She was getting out of the hospital, and I—at least in my memory—stayed and walked out with her before I went back to my Massachusetts job. We made plans for another visit. She would come north to me when she was strong enough. We would imagine this as a future, even if it wasn't quite enough.

I resumed my teaching and talked to her most days, though the thought that she was getting worse, that bad things were going on, and I couldn't stop them, made me occasionally miss calling. It quickly became an awful time for me, when life felt to be edging toward disastrous.

She stayed out of the hospital during that time— September—went for blood transfusions, which made her feel better, but were foreboding. I know she went out with her friends. Had company in. Lived as if life would go on. And then in early October she came to me. I drove to Albany, picked her up, and drove us back to my rented house in Vermont. It was misty. Most of the leaves were down. In the house—an old remodeled barn—it was cold but cheery. I took her out to dinner in Bennington just to get warm. She said she'd had another transfusion for the trip and would stay until its benefits wore off or she became weak again—if that happened.

And that was how we did that. One more kind of regular life between us. I went to campus, did my work, came home nights. She stayed in the big house with my dog. Read books, magazines. Fixed lunches for herself. Watched the Dodgers (this time) beat the Yankees in the Series. Watched Sadat be assassinated. Looked out the window. At night we talked—never serious or worrying things. With Kristina, who was working in New York and commuting on weekends, we went on country drives, looked at antiques, invited visitors, lived together as we had in places far and wide all the years. I didn't know what else we were supposed to do, how else such a time was meant to pass.

On a sunny day in early November, when she had been with me three weeks and we were, in fact, out of things to do and talk about, she sat down beside me on the couch and said, "Richard, I'm not sure how much longer I can look after myself. I'm sorry. But it's just the truth."

"Does it worry you?" I said.

"Well," my mother said, "yes. I'm not scheduled for Presbyterian Village until next year. And I'm not quite sure what I'm going to be able to do until then."

"What would you *like* to do?" I said.

She looked away then, out the window, down the hill, where the trees were bare and fog was shifting. "I don't exactly know," she said.

"Maybe you'll start to feel better," I said.

"Well. Yes. I could. I suppose that's not impossible," she said.

"I think it's possible," I said. "I do."

"Well. OK," my mother said.

"If you don't," I said, "if by Christmas you don't

feel you can do everything for yourself, you can move in with us. I'm going back to Princeton. You can live there."

And I saw in my mother's eyes, then, a light. A *kind* of light, anyway. Recognition. Concession. Willingness. Reprieve of another kind.

"Are you sure about that?" she said and looked at me uncertainly. My mother's eyes were very brown.

"Yes, I'm sure," I said. "You're my mother. I love you."

"Well," she said and nodded, took in a breath, let it out. No tears. "I'll begin to think toward that, then. I'll make some plans about my furniture."

"Well, wait though," I said. And this is a sentence I wish, above all sentences in my life, I had never said. Words I wish I'd never heard. "Don't make your plans yet," I said. "You might feel better by then. It might not be necessary to come to Princeton."

"Oh," my mother said. And whatever had suddenly put a light in her eyes suddenly went away. And her worries resumed. What might lie between now and later rose again. "I see," she said. "All right."

Richard and Edna, East Haven, Vermont, July 4, 1976

I could've not said that. I could've said, "Yes, make your plans. In whatever way all this works out, it'll be just fine. I'll see to it."

But that is what I didn't say. I deferred instead to something else, to some other future, and at least in retrospect I know what that future was. I think she did, too. You *could* say that in those days I had witnessed her facing death, saw it take her nearly out beyond her limits, feared it myself, feared all that I knew, and that I steadfastly clung to the possibility of her life. Or else you could say that I recognized something much more likely. I'll never know for sure. But the truth is that anything we ever could've done for each other after that, passed by in those moments and was gone. Even together we were once again alone.

WHAT REMAINS CAN BE TOLD QUICKLY. In a day or two I drove her back to Albany. She was too cold in my house, she said. She couldn't stay warm, and would be better at home in Little Rock. Though there was not heat enough anywhere to make her warm. She looked pale. When I left her at the airport gate she cried, stood and watched me leaving back up the long corridor. She waved. I waved. It was the last time I would see her that way. On her feet. In the world. We didn't know that. But we knew something was coming.

And in six weeks she was dead. She never got to Princeton. Whatever was wrong with her just took over. "My body's betrayed me" is one thing I remember her saying. Another was, "My chances now are slim and none." And that was true. I came home to Little Rock to sit with her in the hospital, to try to amuse her, remind her of things we'd done, talk to her about my father, ask her to fill in parts of the past—hers and his and theirs—things I didn't know, but which she declined to do as she slipped further away from me into a long, calm sleep, which one day did not end. I never saw her dead. I didn't want to. I simply took the hospital's word when the nurse called early one December morning, just before her birthday.

But, as I said, I saw her face death over and over through that autumn. And because I did, I believe now that witnessing death faced with dignity and courage does not confer either of those—only pity and helplessness and fear. All the rest is just private—moments and messages the world would not be better off to know.

Does one ever have a "relationship" with one's mother? I think not. We—my mother and I—were never bound together by much that was typical, not typical duty, regret, guilt, embarrassment, etiquette. Love, which is never typical, sheltered everything. We expected it to be reliable, and it was. We were always ready to say "I love you," as if a time would come when she would want to hear that, or I would, or that each of us would want to hear ourselves say it to the other, only for some reason—as certainly happened—that would not be possible.

My mother and I look alike. Full, high forehead. Same chin, same nose. There are pictures to show it. In myself I see her, hear her laugh in mine. In her life there was no particular brilliance, no celebrity. No heroics. No one, crowning achievement to swell the heart. There were bad things enough: a childhood that did not bear strict remembering; a husband she loved forever and lost; a life to follow that did not require much comment. But somehow she made possible for me my truest affections, as an act of great literature bestows upon its devoted reader. And I have known that moment with her we would all like to know, the moment of saying, *Yes. This is what it is.* An act of knowing that confirms life's finality and truest worth. I have known that. I have known any number of such moments with her, known them at the instant they occurred, and at this moment as well. I will, I assume, know them forever.

Parker, Richard, and Edna, Jackson, Mississippi, 1945

Afterword

As I said at the beginning, these two memoirs were written thirty years apart. The one regarding my mother was written in the near aftermath of her death, in 1981. The other I wrote only recently, fifty-five years after my father died in 1960. I have placed them in the order found here because records and shared memories of my father's life stretch more deeply into the past than those associated with my mother; whereas my mother's life stretched much further toward the present. The length of their life together and the length of their life with me, and the extent of my mother's life lived alone, have seemed best represented by encountering my father first and my mother second.

I have always admired Auden's poem "La Musée des Beaux Arts" for its acute wisdom that life's most important moments are often barely noticed by others, if noticed at all. Auden's poem considers Brueghel's famous painting *The Fall of Icarus*, in which Icarus is shown floundering in the sea, following his plummet—his fate unobserved by ploughmen tilling their fields on a nearby shore. ". . . Everything turns away," Auden writes, resignedly. Both poem and painting offer their combined visions—rimed with pathos and irony—as an enduring truth of life: the world often doesn't notice us. This understanding has been a crucial urge for most of what I've written in fifty years. Mine has been a life of noticing and being a witness. Most writers' lives are.

The fact that lives and deaths often go unnoticed has specifically inspired this small book about my parents and set its task. Our parents' lives, even those enfolded in obscurity, offer us our first, strong assurance that human events have consequence. *Here we are*, after all. The future is unpredictable and hazardous, but our parents' lives both enact us and help distinguish us. My own belief in lived life's final lack of transcendance always turns me to thoughts of my parents. In difficult moments, long after their deaths, I often experience the purest longing for them—for their actuality. So, to write about them, to *not* turn away, is not only a means to remedy my longing by imagining them near, but is also to point toward that actuality, which—once again—is where my understanding of importance begins.

Has it been my hope to testify to my parents' *lasting-ness*? To their greater-than-obvious importance? In another son's hands, a memoir might do that—try to confer an extra "dimension" where one might not have been evident before. I, however, have tried *not* to make grand claims for my parents. If anything, I've tried to be cautious, so that my own acts of telling about them and their influence on me not distort who they were. I've thus tried, as best I could, to write only about what I factually knew and did not know. My parents were, after all, not made of words. They were not literary instruments *employable* to conjure something larger. Lastingness seems foreign to them and to the sense they had of themselves. If you had known my parents, I'm comfortable you and I could come to different assessments of them. But my hope is that by this writing they would simply be recognizable as the two people I say they were. At day's end, my fondest wish is that my notice of them will ignite thoughts in a reader's mind that my parents can partly, usefully occupy.

I have no children, and what I know of children and childhood and of being a parent, I know almost entirely from being my parents' son. I believe that almost any child, except the most self-involved, perceives his or her parents as separate people— separate from each other and from oneself. For that reason it did not occur to me to write about my parents in any way but as individuals, rather than as a parental "unit." What I didn't anticipate, however, was that as close as they were to one another, how *I* perceive them is much the way they experienced their own lives—as being alone together. All parents must feel this to some extent, since all humans seem to. *Between Them,* this book's title, is meant, in part, to suggest that by being born I literally came between my parents, a virtual place where I was sheltered and adored as long as they were alive. But it is also meant, in part, to portray their ineradicable singleness—both in marriage, and in their lives as my parents.

When people ask me about my childhood I always say, as I've testified above, that I had a wonderful one, and that my parents were wonderful parents. Nothing about this has changed because of this writing. Although what I have come to understand is that within the charmed circumference of "wonderful," that which was most intimate, most important, most satisfying and necessary to each of my parents transpired almost exclusively *between them.* This is not an unhappy fact for a son to face. In most ways it's heartening, since knowing that this is so preserves for me a hopeful mystery about life—the mystery which promises that even with careful notice, much happens that we do not understand.

I have now lived more years than either my

father *or* my mother lived. There is almost no one alive who knew them. And I am, for that reason, the only one who knows these stories and can preserve these memories—at least until now. When I think about my parents after writing about them, I am aware of many things they did and said in my presence and caused to happen that I have not chosen to include here. For instance, why I didn't cry when my father died, and the long-lasting influence of that fact on my life over time. Or, what I suspect to have been the difficult and complex nature of my mother's growing-up in proximity of her colorful but troublesome stepfather. Both of these seem to lead away from my parents, not toward a closer notice of them. But I *can* attest that I have excluded nothing for discretion or propriety's sake, but only because one recollection or another didn't seem important enough, or because a crucial, truthful balance would've been forsaken by including it. John Ruskin wrote that composition is the arrangement of unequal things. Thus the chore for the memoir writer is to compose a shape and an economy that gives faithful, reliable, if sometimes drastic, coherence to the many unequal things any life contains. As I have already, repeatedly said, humans comprise much more than anyone can tell about them. And as for living so long without my parents, all I can say is that the rueful injustice of not having them close to me for more of my life is a far less significant injustice than the one done to *them*—being forced to leave life early, so long before they could've grown tired of it.

A friend said to me recently that to him my parents' lives—lives you've now read about—seem sad. But, setting aside their relative brevity, my parents' lives do not seem sad to me, nor do I believe they themselves would have thought that sadness characterized their days. There *was* sadness. But when they were together, including when I was with them (and often because of it), their life—I believe—seemed to them better than any life they could've expected, given how and where they'd begun. To say what this "better" life amounted to is in some ways a light I have tried to shed. Writing these two remembrances, indeed, has been a source of immense exhilaration for me—quite different from what I would've expected, given the longing I often experience. I was fortunate to have parents who loved each other and, out of the crucible of that great, almost unfathomable love, loved me. Love, as always, confers beauties.

Finally, in totaling up the reasons to write a memoir, there must be admitted the *me* part that is alloyed into the middle of all I've told—*my* needs, for *my* purposes, enforcing *my* version of good sense and continuity between today and long ago—my urge to reconcile my self-back-then when my parents were alive, with my self-now, decades after they've died. The memoirist is never just the teller of other people's stories, but is a character in those stories. So, to write about my parents long after they've gone inevitably discloses hollow places, failures, frailties, rents and absences in me, insufficiencies that the telling, itself, may have tried to put right or seal off, but may only have re-opened and left behind, absences that no amount of life or truthful telling can completely fill or conceal. These I agree to live with. Though when I turn to regard life—my own or others'—I now never fail to be struck, amid the onslaught of all that's happened and still is happening, by how much that's gone from me. Absences seem to surround and intrude upon everything. Though in acknowledging this, I cannot let it be a loss or even be a fact I regret, since that is merely how life is—another enduring truth we must notice.

Acknowledgments

I owe great thanks to my friends Geoffrey Wolff, Blake Morrison, Michael Ondaatje, Mary Karr, Joyce Carol Oates, and to the incomparable Eudora Welty, who in writing so affectingly about their parents, have provided models for me and made such writing seem both feasible and possibly useful.

I wish also to acknowledge and thank my loved ones both present and gone, who over years and against odds have made me realize that I am part of a large and embracing family. These relations include my late aunt Viva Haney; my cousins Elizabeth Fay and Carrol Wayne Norris; my cousins Emmett Carrol and Bobbie Jean Haney, Jim and Barbara Horton; and my more distant but precious cousins, the late Euleta and W. J. Bowden; their daughter, Mary Prewitt; her husband, Dr. Taylor Prewitt, and their son, Kendrick, and his wife, Dr. Lindsey Prewitt. I must also remember the Gibson girls, Elizabeth Hickman, Margaret Helen Cheek, and Bessie Fengler, in observance of their years of loving friendship to me and to Kristina, and to my mother. I remember also, with love, my late Uncle Buster—S. E. Shelley—who came to the fore, unasked.

I am grateful to Inge Feltrinelli, Carlo Feltrinelli, and to Tomás Maldonado, for generously providing a room and a table in Villadeati, where I could finish this book.

I wish to thank Dale Rohrbaugh, Bridget Read, Leisha MacDougall, and Jennifer Field for their indispensable acumen and friendship in times of need.

I wish as well to thank my enduring friend Daniel Halpern who edited this book with sensitivity and grace. And I wish to thank Amanda Urban for her decades of never-flagging, never-uninteresting, and loving comradeship—which continues. My gratitude, as well, to Patricia Towers, who long ago encouraged me to write about my mother. And my undiminished gratitude to Ben Wilson, M.D., for his empathy, candor and uncommon decency, many years ago now.

And last, my thanks to Kristina Ford, for simply everything. RF